Knockout job interview presentations

How to present with confidence, beat the competition and impress your way into a top job

Rebecca Corfield

KoganPage

LONDON   PHILADELPHIA   NEW DELHI

First published in Great Britain and the United States in 2010 by Kogan Page Limited

120 Pentonville Road	525 South 4th Street, #241	4737/23 Ansari Road
London N1 9JN	Philadelphia PA 19147	Daryaganj
United Kingdom	USA	New Delhi 110002
www.koganpage.com		India

© Rebecca Corfield, 2010

The right of Rebecca Corfield to be identified as the author of this work has been asserted by her in accordance with the Copyright, Designs and Patents Act 1988.

ISBN 978 0 7494 5715 0
E-ISBN 978 0 7494 5925 3

British Library Cataloguing-in-Publication Data

A CIP record for this book is available from the British Library.

Library of Congress Cataloging-in-Publication Data

Corfield, Rebecca.
    Knockout job interview presentations : how to present with confidence, beat the competition and impress your way into a top job / Rebecca Corfield.
        p. cm.
    ISBN 978-0-7494-5715-0 -- ISBN 978-0-7494-5925-3 (ebk) 1. Employment interviewing. 2. Job hunting. I. Title.
    HF5549.5.I6C68 2010
    650.14'4--dc22
                                        2009033397

Typeset by Saxon Graphics, Derby
Printed and bound in India by Replika Press Pvt Ltd

Contents

About the author

In her late 20s Rebecca trained as a careers adviser, learning how career choices are made and how we take decisions about our lives. It is often as adults that we first start to think more seriously about where we are going. She has run organizations that help all ages of people to re-train and find jobs. Often her clients would need encouragement as well as new skills. Rebecca worked with groups on CV preparation, filling in application forms and on interview techniques. She trained as an image consultant, specifically so that she could advise jobseekers on the best way to present themselves at interview.

Rebecca was President of the Institute of Career Guidance – the national professional organization for careers advisers in the UK. She started the National Careers Awards to highlight the best work that was being done in the profession. Over 10 years later, these prestigious awards are still presented every year and are sponsored by *The Independent*.

Over time Rebecca has collated a wealth of experience from the labour market. Employers ask her to help with employing and selecting staff – in advising them how to recruit and retain the best people for each specific place of work. Keeping staff productive and happy needs a clear picture of where you are going, an understanding of what makes people 'tick', and clear communication.

Rebecca has often worked with staff who are to lose their jobs, giving group and individual advice about how to start anew in the jobs market. The best careers advice can really change your life. The right guidance is important when you are a jobseeker, but so also is support and motivation, and knowing that you are not on your own in trying to make progress.

People seek Rebecca out at times of crisis, for coaching and when decisions have to be made. From the most senior people running national institutions or from those in business, the arts or politics, the requests for help cover the same needs as for the young school or college leaver: they seek guidance to improve the impact they have on other people; to learn the secret of structuring their presentations and tips on how to handle nerves. They all want feedback on how they come across when standing up to speak.

On her travels, Rebecca has found that the pressures we face are the same from Asia across to Europe. Getting a job – at every level – needs confidence, clarity of vision and enthusiasm. Making presentations is as nerve-racking for the new entrant to the job market as for the CEO to the Board.

What Rebecca has to say can make a significant difference. That is why she writes her books – to spread her advice about how to get ahead, to help you see what recruiters are looking for and how you can demonstrate the special contribution you can make. All the knowledge she has gained from employers, employees and jobseekers is distilled into her writing so that you can read, understand and act on her advice, to advance your own career prospects.

Rebecca has three books published by Kogan Page: *Preparing the Perfect CV*, *Successful Interview Skills* and *Preparing the Perfect Job Application*, all now in new 5th editions.

Introduction

You have an interview coming up. You are excited because it represents the gateway to getting a new job that could change your life. You know about the job and will be happy to give the interview your best shot. There's just one small snag: something stands in the way of you and success. The invitation letter has said that you need to give a presentation as part of the interview. You have been asked to talk on a given subject for a specific amount of time, before your interview starts. The panel will evaluate your performance as part of your overall score at the interview.

This is not an uncommon occurrence. More and more employers ask candidates to give a presentation at their job interview. You could be given the subject of the presentation in advance or you may only be told the topic on the day. Your heart sinks as you realize that you will have to stand up and speak on a topic of the panel's choosing whilst they scrutinize you from every aspect.

Why giving a presentation can be so scary

For around 10 to 15 minutes, you are going to have to talk before a group of strangers. You will have to impress them and convince them that you are the best candidate for the job by standing up and presenting your material to them. For some reason this seems much more scary than just sitting across a table being interviewed.

For the duration of your presentation the panel will be completely focused on you. They will be analysing your every move, dissecting each sentence and judging your potential, whilst eyeing you critically from top-to-toe. Your success at giving the presentation will form a major part of the way that you are assessed as suitable for the job. There is always more than one candidate in competition for every vacancy and employers may have lots of applicants for certain jobs. To help them decide which person to give the job to, they will up the stakes so that they can weed out the less able candidates.

Asking candidates to give a presentation allows them to compare and contrast the different applicants. The panel will be looking at all aspects of the presentation: the way the material has been put together; the amount of preparation that has been involved, the delivery of the presentation, and the impact it achieves.

This book contains the secrets of making a successful presentation to enhance your impact at an interview. You will have the advantage over other job candidates and will be able to make a presentation with the ease and confidence to trump the competition. It contains advice and quotations from people who have had to do all kinds of presentations in interviews; with employers and recruiters about how they select staff, and from HR experts on what employers are looking for from a presentation.

There are rules for putting together effective presentations which have impact and impress employers. Employers use presentations for specific reasons, therefore careful planning is required: by thinking about the audience; how to communicate best with them; thorough preparation, and delivery with style. Thorough preparation pays dividends, and structuring what is to be said leads to success. All questions about how to organize presentations are covered in full.

Why we lack confidence and how we acquire it

Feelings of nervousness can create anxiety, if you know that a lack of confidence and fear of speaking in public could affect your job chances:

○ You may be worrying in case you will get an interview with a presentation as part of it.

○ You may know that you have to do a presentation for the kind of job you want but lack the confidence or the skills to tackle this.

○ You may have had to do presentations at previous interviews and feel you failed in this task, or did not impress the panel, and did not get offered the job – you don't want this to be repeated.

○ It may be that you are a fairly confident presenter in your day job, but you would like to refresh yourself with the key elements of what matters in giving presentations in an interview situation.

Nerves can be controlled and conquered.

Planning and demystifying

Many of us are not sure how to plan for a job interview with a presentation as a major part of it. Even if you have had to do presentations as part of your regular job, you may not fully understand what will be expected of you in this respect in an interview; you are not sure what employers want to hear in a speech delivered to a brief. Even more alarming, you may be asked to speak off the cuff with no prior notice. You will be wondering how to target the presentation to the audience, especially if you are an internal candidate for a promotion post. You want to know how to get your points across without waffling and how to use the interview to really sell yourself.

It can seem to be a mystery what style to use as a presenter. Only the candidate who is confident and impressive in making a presentation will get the job. We can all do with some advice about how to be humorous and how to strike the right note. Knowing how to gain authority can be a big advantage, especially for a senior or promotion post, but often at the same time, we also need to come across as accessible.

Knowing how to gain involvement and audience participation is tricky even if it can enliven a presentation. Responding to questions at the end of your presentation seems daunting and you may worry about coming under attack, sounding defensive or having nothing to say. You want advice about preparation and using notes and visual aids. More than anything you need tips on handling nerves, being assertive, and controlling body language. You want to know how to handle nightmare situations and what to do if problems arise in a presentation.

This book will answer all these questions. Having to do a presentation as part of your interview is not to be feared but welcomed. Knowing that you have to make a presentation gives you a huge advantage. It is as good as knowing the questions that you are going to be asked in advance of an exam. You can prepare exactly the right answer to the topic that you have been given and you can choose how to order, feature and present your information. Just think what an advantage that gives you over an interview with no presentation as part of it.

Passing on my experiences

My expertise ranges from working with complete beginners, to very senior clients – in the public sector, politics and the business world – and I have taught presentation skills for over 20 years. I have often assessed clients giving presentations in interviews and have advised employers how to structure interviews to include presentations, and how to judge these.

Candidates who come to the interview pleased that they have a chance to present their material and confident about the way that they are going to come across, are often winners. *You* can catch that positive feeling too. All the examples and case studies in this book are taken and adapted from real stories from people I have met, trained or interviewed – my thanks go to them for that inspiration.

Would you like to feel more secure and be successful? You will know everything there is to know about presentations as part of the selection process. You will have the power to choose what to do to gain the perception you are looking for in the panel. After reading this book you will be more likely to be one of the lucky ones. Read on.

How to use this book

The secrets of how to give knockout presentations can be found here. If you have a presentation to do soon in an interview, you may want to read the book from cover to cover so that you acquire all the knowledge it contains – particularly if it is the first time that you have to present material as part of an interview; you will be keen to get tips and hints to make yourself successful. If you are refreshing your knowledge on the topic, you may just want to browse through the book then revisit it again the next time an interview with a presentation crops up.

This book may be of help to you if you have a history of not being very confident at giving any kind of presentation. Perhaps you have had to present at work and have not enjoyed it, or you have had feedback that indicates you could do with some improvement. This book will give you lots of ideas about how to perform under pressure. You may be an adviser to others who have to undergo presentations during interviews. This book will give you the whole picture about how best to help your clients.

Chapter summaries

Every chapter has three areas to note:

○ First are the Dos and Don'ts in each one. These are hints – things to try and to apply, and things to avoid.

○ The second area is Points to Remember – key elements from each chapter to retain for the future.

○ The third is the Knockout Tips from the chapters – the real winning contributions. They are shown by this sign:

Knockout Tip!

You will find the essential tip highlighted here. If you only take away one thing from each chapter, this should be it.

Chapter 1: The basics

The main features of this book relate to creating and maintaining a positive outlook – generating the feeling that you can do this. In Chapter 1 we will look in detail at why employers have presentations as part of the interview process and what are they looking for. It covers what we all want from our job interview presentation experience and explores why we lack the necessary confidence and how we can acquire it.

Being taken notice of and heard, being direct and coming over as an interesting person are totally necessary. You need to be able to stick to the point and get your message and vision across and be able to speak off the cuff. Even if you know the topic of your presentation, you will often have to speak without notes, for example, when being asked questions at the end of your session.

Selling yourself often feels like the biggest challenge as you battle with your nerves. We need to get motivated so that we channel our energy into gaining respect from an audience. Overall we want to find the key to unlock the treasure of what we know.

Chapter 2: Planning

Chapter 2 covers all aspects of planning your interview presentation, knowing what to include and how to organize it. We will analyse what makes a good presentation so we can see what we are aiming for. We will think about presentations where you know the topic, and those where you go in without any prior notice of the subject being given.

We will examine working to the brief or title that you have been given, looking at different kinds of brief, and covering how to best plan for each type. The main aim of planning is to decide what to say. We cover researching the correct information – including how to tackle new subjects and how to plan for any questions you may receive; the chapter gives aids to creative thinking that can be invaluable for this. We will cover using humour as part of your plan.

You need to plan for the specific type and size of the audience. A big decision is to accurately gauge the level and style of presentation; you need to have a certain amount of authority, depending on what kind of job you are going for, but you also need to come over as accessible and open. If you are being interviewed for an internal vacancy, you need to know how to pitch your presentation to familiar colleagues and managers.

Chapter 3: Preparation

In Chapter 3 we take a look at all the aspects of preparation – the practical aspects of getting everything ready. The first and key lesson here is about how to structure your presentation – which is as relevant here as for any kind of presentation. Accurately assessing the correct timing is key to creating a good impression. No panel will be impressed by a misjudgement of this element.

Talking to your audience and making that vital connection with them can be tricky, particularly when you have to deal with people that you know in the audience, for example, if you are going for an internal vacancy. Talking to strangers takes nerve too and we will look at how you put all this together. It may be appropriate to your subject to elicit audience participation and we will look at some examples of how to do this. We cover using different types of prompt notes, and evaluate the visual aids and props that you could include. Rehearsing is a big part of getting prepared and we also cover how to prepare to answer questions.

Chapter 4: Presentation

Getting it right on the day is explored in Chapter 4, which discusses presentation; the most difficult part can be actually delivering your presentation. How to handle the inevitable nerves will be discussed, by understanding what feeling nervous is all about. You will see that you can stay calm, stand your ground and have impact if you follow the advice given. There will be times when the unexpected happens so we also explore thinking on your feet, to cope with these moments.

'Delivery' involves using your personal image to create authority whilst still giving a natural performance. You need to know how to use facial expressions and body language to your advantage. Handling nerves is the topic we need most help with in this chapter. How to cope with distractions and knowing how to handle your emotions involves maintaining control and putting a stop to the voice of self-criticism within. We discuss being assertive – or at least faking it – by knowing how to look composed on the outside.

Chapter 5: Learning and improving

No one is an expert right from the word go. Chapter 5 covers learning and improving. Presentation skills are something on which you can build all your life. You can evaluate your presentations in a variety of ways so that you build learning into your experience over time. In this chapter we look at how to get feedback on your style to monitor the quality of your presentations as well as how to do the same for friends and colleagues.

If presentation skills are for life – as part of your job and future career – then you may appreciate some tips for moving on in your speaking career. This could involve speaking to bigger audiences and work conferences; participating more in meetings, seminars etc, and using chairing skills, all of which are covered in this chapter.

Chapter 6: Facing tricky situations

Even the most thorough preparation can't predict every difficult situation that can arise. Disasters do happen and a selection of tricky issues is covered in the questions and answers section in Chapter 6. Finding yourself in front of the panel from hell, coping with scepticism, and people trying to undermine you are all looked at. Here you can find the answers to overcoming hurdles, handling nightmare situations, and dealing with interruptions, challenges and conflict.

Conclusion

The Conclusion sums up the contents of the book and provides you with a step-by-step guide to giving a knockout presentation in your interview. Further sources of help from Kogan Page are provided at the end of the book.

Inside these pages you will discover a pragmatic guide to giving a knockout presentation as part of your job interview. Presentations at interview are now a fact of life and you are bound to come across them in your career – don't let your lack of confidence or knowledge of them be an obstacle any longer. Nerves and lack of experience can be overcome. Take control of your future and get ready to embrace success.

The basics

This chapter looks in detail at why employers decide to have presentations as part of the interview process and what they are looking for when they do. It is also important to think through what we want to learn about presentations of this type and why we sometimes lack confidence in ourselves. We shall then go on to consider the ideal image we would like to project when delivering our presentation.

Why presentations are used in interviews

Let's start by looking at why employers choose to have presentations as part of their recruitment process.

Interviews are not a particularly scientific way of obtaining staff. There are no guarantees that the person who appears confident and winning across the interview desk will be excellent as an employee. It is easy to make a good impression when you are just sitting down and chatting in the abstract about how you would do a job. You can make all sorts of claims about your abilities and personality, which may or may not be true.

As a result, employers want to have a more rigorous method of testing candidates to see who performs better in a more real-life situation. In an attempt to find out more about candidates, and to help them pick the best person, they will often add other activities: a role play, an in-tray exercise, a discussion group or… making candidates do a presentation.

Employers' reasons for choosing to have a presentation

I asked employers for their top 10 reasons for having a presentation as part of a candidate's interview process. Here are the results:

1. To test knowledge about a specific area of the job description.

2. To cover one of the big job areas in advance of the interview.

3. To elicit a candidate's own views in some detail.

4. To see how well they can handle and talk to a brief.

5. To see how well candidates can communicate their thoughts.

6. To see how thoroughly and cleverly they can prepare in advance.

7. To see how candidates bear up under the pressure of having to 'perform'.

8. To see how candidates deal with a presentation on the day, without prior notice.

9. To see how persuasive and interesting candidates are in front of an audience.

10. To see how candidates interact with an audience, and deal with questions.

Let us look at each of these in turn:

1. To test knowledge about a specific area of the job description

Getting the candidate to do a presentation on one area of the job description enables a more detailed insight into the way each candidate sees the job. An example of such a presentation could be, 'Explain how you would manage this finance department'.

In their presentations, Candidate A might concentrate on checking mechanisms, thorough systems and tight overall monetary control, focusing on the smaller details and processes; Candidate B might stress staff management, interdepartmental communications and accessible management statistics, concentrating on the bigger picture. Neither would necessarily be wrong but there would be an apparent difference in approach to the job as a result of the presentation, before the interview had even started.

By setting a presentation on an area of the job, the employer replaces the need for such a long interview by finding out in your 10-minute presentation what might take half an hour of interviewing to elicit.

One employer said: 'It gives a good steer on how the applicants see the job. We can then move to question them in the interview to back up our understanding of where they are coming from, or to check out their attitude to other elements of the job they seem not to have taken into account.'

2. To cover one of the big job areas in advance of the interview

Some presentations can ask the candidate about an area of the job that is of overriding importance. For instance, in an interview for a marketing job, a large part of the interview will need to be about the candidate's knowledge and experience of marketing. By asking candidates to give a presentation such as: 'Tell us about your experience in marketing' or 'Describe how you would approach managing the marketing function in this organization', the panel will be able to cover this important area of the job during the presentation. This gets a substantial area of questioning out of the way through the presentation and enables the panel to spend the subsequent interview asking about other areas of the job.

One employer commented: 'Most of the candidates will be competent in the main aspects of the job or they wouldn't have been called for interview. If we get the point of the job out of the way in the presentation then we can spend the questioning period asking about the other factors such as how they work in a team, their attitude to management, how they see the future priorities etc. It means we can focus much more on finding out about the individuals before us in the interview.'

3. To elicit a candidate's own views in some detail

A question such as, 'Where do you think we should be going with our product development?' asks candidates to put forward their views on a topic that they have had a chance to think about, enabling their answer to be contrasted with those of other candidates. The views, opinions and expertise of each can be assessed by the way they answer the question.

Another employer observed: 'It is remarkable how much people reveal in a presentation. It can be quite clear which candidates' views chime with ours by the elements they choose to talk about. With some we are nodding in agreement all the way through their presentation, with others it is difficult to find any areas of common ground.'

The basics ■ 15

4. To see how well they can handle and talk to a brief

Being given a topic on which to present can be difficult. It involves you in taking stock, planning your approach, dealing with your nerves on the day and focusing on the message you wish to convey. Putting all this together is no mean feat. Even if you plan well, you may fail to deliver in the way you want.

Public speaking forms a part of many jobs. Some roles are frequently involved with speaking to groups of people, for example, jobs in Public Relations, and the training of staff or marketing executives. Even if you don't have to present to clients or customers, many other jobs require occasional presentations to be made to team members, visitors or to groups of colleagues. Also, any managerial or supervisory job will involve you in talking to groups of staff regularly.

One recruiter described it this way: 'If candidates can put together a good presentation in the interview we will have confidence in them to be able to carry out this function in the job if they get it. Quite often in our work we need to convey information to others about our products and that is why we ask for a demonstration of this skill in the interview.'

5. To see how well candidates can communicate their thoughts

Planning a brilliant presentation will not in itself be enough to get you through. You need to be able to translate your thoughts on a given topic into an entertaining and pithy presentation so that it can be heard and appreciated by your audience.

One recruitment specialist shares this point: 'I often don't really follow what the candidates are trying to say. Presumably *they* know what they mean but it doesn't always come over clearly at all to the audience, and unless they can do that, they have not really communicated with me.'

6. To see how thoroughly and cleverly they can prepare in advance

Researching a topic, organizing your material and then compiling a presentation is a complex, creative process. Motivating yourself to put your presentation together takes attention to detail and enthusiasm for your topic.

A human resources manager told me: 'Intelligent, confident candidates often come a cropper doing their presentations because they think they will be able to wing it on the day. This is a bad idea. It comes over really clearly when someone hasn't prepared properly. The material is often too much or too little, their thoughts don't flow in a sensible order and it is clear that they have left out some areas completely.'

7. To see how candidates bear up under the pressure of having to 'perform'

Even when you are fully prepared, the pressure of the actual event can prove distracting at best, and at worst, totally impossible to handle. Learning how to overcome feelings of nervousness on the day is vital.

One businesswoman said: 'I do feel sorry for people who get all nervy and crack under the pressure but there's no way I am going to employ them. I need people who are the opposite of that – people who enjoy the attention, like holding the floor and delivering their presentation and who come out all guns blazing.'

8. To see how candidates deal with a presentation on the day, without prior notice

Sometimes you are only given the topic for your presentation on the day. All the candidates have to prepare their topic at the interview itself and some time will be given for this –

often half an hour to an hour in total. How you react to having to give your presentation with only a short amount of preparation tells the employer how calm you can be at turning round a presentation in such a short time.

One senior manager confided: 'In our work we are often up on platforms having to defend the position of the local authority. Anything and everything can be thrown at you and you just have to be able to think, react and deliver in a cool, confident way. A presentation topic only given on the day is a good test of how well candidates know their stuff and can defend their ground.'

9. To see how persuasive and interesting candidates are in front of an audience

Having a speech written does not necessarily mean that it will be of interest to other people. On a topic where you need to persuade people to a certain course of action, both the words spoken, the argument followed and the delivery all play their part in having an effect.

One Sales Manager said: 'I am only going to employ the most persuasive people so I am not looking for someone nice or cuddly. I need someone who will knock me off my feet with their presentation. I know that if they can sell themselves to me, they will be able to sell our products with ease.'

10. To see how candidates interact with an audience, and deal with questions

Giving a presentation is not just about delivering the content; it also involves picking up clues and cues from the audience, adjusting and tailoring what you are saying as a result, and then dealing with the points raised by the audience at the end. This can mean thinking on your feet all over again as the questions are fired at you for your response.

A senior manager said: 'Dealing with customer queries and complaints forms a lot of our work so the rapport that the candidates build with the audience and the way that they cope with the questions at the end of the presentation can tell us just as much as what they talked to us about in their presentation in the first place.'

Qualities of a good speaker

Let us start by thinking about what characteristics are shared by good speakers. If we can identify those characteristics it may help us to learn how to make use of some of those same factors.

Who are the speakers whom you rate highly? When we are asked to name speakers with impact, we often think of political figures such as Tony Blair, Nelson Mandela and Barack Obama. Sometimes we think of charismatic people from the past such as Mahatma Gandhi, Winston Churchill or Adolf Hitler, who could hold a crowd with their oratory.

Other people who spring to mind are entertainers or TV presenters who pull in and attract audiences, with their ability to take the floor and keep our attention.

Here are the results of a large survey I have carried out with students on presentation skills courses. When asked what makes a good speaker this is what they said:

○ Someone who has: authority and control; leadership qualities; confidence; robust presence; power; reputation, and who is worthy of respect.

○ Speakers who: issue a call to action; make an appeal; motivate us; are persuasive; are empowering; are making a difference; show results; show shared values; can involve us; make connections; are direct; have a vision.

○ A person who: uses structure; has appropriate pace and use of pauses; has timing; uses material that is targeted to the audience; is focused and clear; shows clarity of message.

○ Someone exhibiting a relaxed attitude, and having an open manner and accessible style.

○ Someone who is: showing enthusiasm; enjoying themselves; not making the presentation a chore; not dreading it.

○ A speaker who is: interesting; satisfying; entertaining; funny; using humour; giving a performance.

○ A speaker who: shows knowledge; knows their subject; knows their stuff; has the answers; gives us factual content.

○ Someone with: positive body language; a nice appearance; good grooming; charm; smooth delivery; an impressive visual image; good eye contact and a varied voice.

○ Speakers who: have energy; are passionate; speak from the heart; seem to be one of us; are sincere; have charisma; we can relate to; seem human; are honest; appear fallible.

○ Speakers that can be: controversial; putting points across and convincing; provocative; individualistic; rousing; doing it differently; taking risks.

It takes all sorts. We can see from this list of bullet points that there is no one stereotype of a brilliant presenter. None of the famous political leaders or TV presenters exhibit all of these characteristics, however brilliant they may be. There are as many good speakers and presenters as there are personality types. This is good news as it means that there is room for all of us to be ourselves and yet still come over well when we take the floor.

What we all want

So if that covers the impressive characteristics that we see in other people, what do we want for ourselves?

In the same survey I asked people to rank the aspects that they most wanted to learn, about giving presentations. These were the results. See how they compare with what you feel are your needs.

Confidence

Confidence is the first and most important attribute that people say they want.

'I want more guts! I need to stop my endless self-criticism that holds me back', said one woman. We want to feel an end to the fearful feelings that allow nerves to get the better of us.

'I want to be able to relax and enjoy myself, or at least have enough composure to fake it until I feel better.' 'I never feel in control of what is happening.' 'I would like to be more assertive in my delivery.' 'I have some great things to say but I need to be taken notice of and I know that is down to me to make them hear me properly.' 'I want to switch them on through my excellent content.'

Planning

Putting an interesting speech together is not easy. This is how one man puts it: 'I find it really difficult to get my message over. I know I come across as too formal and sound dull. I think it must all be in the planning. I need to know how to structure my presentation to pitch it at the right level so that I bond with my audience more instead of just boring them. Ideally I would like to make my presentations more varied.'

Presentation

Another said, 'Selling myself is the difficult bit for me. I don't feel I have charisma, and trying to perform and have impact whilst also coming over as natural seems quite a contradiction. I'm not confident about my image and need to know more about using facial expression and body language. I just curl up and die inside at the thought of having all those strangers examining my performance.'

A young woman added, 'I plan everything fine but then go completely off the point and start waffling hopelessly. I seem to lose the momentum to carry on through the planned presentation and then the timing goes out of the window and they ask me to stop because my time is up when I am only half way through.'

Handling difficulties

Dealing with people you know in the audience can be hard. One man said: 'I have tried three times to get an internal promotion. Of course, I know the people interviewing me and that's why I go to pieces. It is a real nightmare when I know full well they know all about me and can see right through my claims.'

Another woman said, 'The presentation usually goes OK, but it is when they ask me probing questions that I get into trouble. If I haven't prepared the material I just flounder and dry up and it must look dreadful.'

Learning and improving

It is common to get stuck in a performance rut with regard to presentations. One woman confided, 'I keep going for interviews and I know that the presentation is what is letting me down. I never seem to get any better or more confident and I am desperate to get some objective feedback so I can improve.'

Career development

Another man added, 'I want to get better at presentations, partly to improve my success in interviews but also for the sake of my career more generally. I would love to be able to speak in public whenever the need arose; to feel confident in front of bigger audiences so I can make my mark.'

Once, in a training course I was running, one of the delegates summed up what everyone wanted: 'All we want is to unlock the treasure of what we know.' How true this statement is. We all want to wow the employer into giving us the job. What we all want from our job interview presentation is to come over as the candidate with the most to offer.

We can lack the necessary confidence when we have to make that presentation. Confidence is a funny business. We don't necessarily know it is there but we certainly notice when it isn't.

Take driving a car for instance. It all happens every time we get in the vehicle, but that is a very different situation to when we first learned to drive. Then, every gear change, look in the mirror and manoeuvre was difficult and awkward. What made the difference? Practice mainly. Plus being taught by a professional and then tested by an objective outsider.

We can replicate that process with giving presentations. The main element of feeling more confident is having done it before. Don't leave it to the day itself to perform for the first time. You need to get in as much practice as you can and do lots of rehearsing. Just like an actor, this is what enables you to feel confident that it will be all right on the night.

Being taken notice of and heard, being direct and interesting are all things we desire. You need to be able to stick to the point and get your message and vision across, and be able to speak off the cuff. Even if you know the topic of your presentation, you will often have to speak without notes when being asked questions at the end of your session.

What employers always want

And what about what employers are looking for from candidates when they recruit using a presentation? (The points are in random order; the numbers do not indicate priority.)

1. Stating clearly what contribution they can make.

2. Good first impressions; clean and well groomed.

3. Body language; confidence; independence.

4. Communication.

5. Preparation; evidence they have done their homework.

6. Positive enthusiasm and interests.

7. Transferable skills; matching skills.

8. Complement team; fitting in.

9. Handling pressure; handling conflicting priorities.

10. Love of learning; adaptable and willing.

Knockout Tip!

It is what you are offering to bring to the workplace that will make the employer want to give you the job.

Let us consider each of the above in turn as they are all things to try to convey or bring out in your presentation, to make that good impression.

1. Stating clearly what contribution they can make

This is what will get you the job over the other candidates. So often I hear applicants for a job talking about why they want the job, how beneficial it will be for their career, how if fits in with their life right now, and so on. I feel like saying: 'Stop right there! This is of little or no interest to those of us sitting on the panel listening to you. Everyone who is making a presentation to us wants this job for similar reasons as yours. But what are you offering us? If you can just see this from our point of view you would not talk about what you would get from us hiring you but focus instead on what you would bring to the organization or company.'

2. Good first impressions

You don't need to buy clothes or go mad on beauty treatments, just make sure that you spend time on what you are going to wear and look like, so that you look clean and well-groomed and that you have tried hard to impress the panel. Tie your hair back if it gets in the way, flops over your face or if you are tempted to twiddle with it all the time. Remove over-exuberant jewellery and keep the clothes plain, suitable and smart.

3. Body language

One employer said: 'We are looking for confident, independent people. We don't need them to look any particular way, just that they stand tall, can shake hands, smile in greeting us and overcome those feelings of nervousness that we expect them to have.'

4. Communication

Can you talk to people clearly and directly? That is one of the things the panel will be assessing. You do not need to be a technical wizard or a brilliant orator, you just need to be able to convey your ideas effectively.

5. Preparation

One of the main points of asking for a presentation is to see evidence that candidates have done their homework in preparing for the day.

6. Positive enthusiasm

'A positive attitude shines through and makes me want to employ that person', said one Director of a major charity. 'If they have a bit of bounce and passion about them, I know they will stay interested even when the going gets tough.'

7. Transferable skills

Most employers don't need you to have the exact basket of skills that are needed for the job, but the more you have experience of the kind of work they are offering – or skills that are similar – the easier it will be for them to imagine you in the job. They will know that it will be a fairly good fit between what you know now and what you will need to know to do the job well.

8. Complement team

Employers are looking for people who will fit in with their existing workforce. One supervisor put it: 'I don't want an identikit clone but I am not going to employ someone who will upset or antagonize my current team. If a person looks helpful, keen and co-operative, that goes a long way.'

9. Handling pressure

The ability to stay strong and calm under pressure means that you could be relied upon to deal with all sorts of difficulties such as handling conflicting priorities and surviving a crisis.

10. Love of learning

If you can introduce into your presentation some evidence of being adaptable and keen to learn this will always earn you bonus points. There are not many jobs where you can just stand still with your existing knowledge, so a willingness to pick up new skills and aptitudes will be attractive.

Creating the perception you want

One of the exciting aspects of going for a job interview is the chance to subtly reinvent yourself. In a new role in a new organization (or a new role in the same place if it is an internal vacancy) you will act differently and as a result you can decide anew how you want to come across. You will have learned a lot in your present job and each new stage of your career sees you learn and grow. Each time you move on, you are a slightly different person and you need the perception you create to accurately reflect this growth and development.

External perceptions

Do you have any idea of the way other people perceive you? Current colleagues and friends will certainly have an impression of you. It may be all good and you may be perfectly happy with the way you come across. In that case all you need to do is make sure that you represent yourself accurately in your presentation and interview. You may know how you are seen by others but want to change this in some way, either because it is incorrect or because you would like to add things to that perception.

Have you ever been surprised to find that people think you are a certain character that you do not think is true yourself? You may be seen as remote and stand-offish when all you feel is shy and self-conscious. You may be seen as competent and a safe pair of hands but want to be seen as more of a risk-taker and innovator. Do people think you are a snappy dresser; a cool character; a nice person but without much spark; reliable and a safe pair of hands or a maverick who is unpredictable?

Platform for change

You may have had managers' comments or performance reviews in the past where you have been assessed as under-performing in some way and you now want to set the record straight. You may have made mistakes and now want the credit for trying to make changes even if they didn't come off. In any event, you need to know how others see you before you can think of altering this perception.

You could ask people you trust to give you some tips on how they think you could try to alter your image to help you to come over better during the interview presentation.

Try the following exercise. See if you can remember if you have been described in a certain way in job reports, assessments, or performance reviews. Have you ever had feedback from interviews where you were not successful, where they told you what their impressions of you were? Were there any aspects of the way you came across that surprised you, perhaps because you were not aware of giving out that impression? Maybe they thought you were quiet and shy when in fact inside you felt confident, or they thought you were a safe pair of hands when you were actually full of new and innovative ideas.

Exercise

Look at these lists of words that could be used for a character description. Do you think any might be applied to you at the moment?

Calm	Laid-back	Friendly
Excitable	Safe	Reserved
Outgoing	Risky	Loud
Introverted	Thoughtful	Quiet
Reflective	Impulsive	Chatty
Action-oriented	Cool	Private
Smart	Passionate	Confident
Scruffy	Emotional	Shy
Casual	Rational	Giver
Formal	Assertive	Taker
Dull	Passive	Innovative
Exciting	Leader	Conservative
Hardworking	Follower	Practical

Using words from the lists above – or any other words that seem appropriate – write down in the space below, the way that you think you are perceived by others. If your bosses were asked to write a reference for you today, what would they be likely to say? Think back through past references, appraisal summaries or feedback you have had for comments that have been made. Include, also, perceptions that you have heard from friends, family and colleagues; if you have time, you could ask this group for their current input, so it's up to date.

Good points:

_____

_____

_____

_____

_____

Now carry on with this self-analysis by thinking of any negative perceptions that may exist of you. What areas might others say, that needed developing in you? Have you ever had any criticisms made about you in the past? Even if you don't agree with them, write them below.

Less good points:

_____

_____

_____

_____

_____

Now take a long hard look at what you have come up with. Is this a perception that will take you into a new job? Does it perhaps have some elements missing that you think any new employer might be looking for? Are there any words there that you think you would rather not be looking at? Perhaps there are perceptions of your character that are now out of date or from which you want to move on.

Are there any aspects of the perception of you that you would like to encourage? The presentation at the interview is you showing yourself off at your best. What could you try to show or demonstrate that perhaps no one has seen in you before? How do you secretly see yourself at your best?

The perception I would like to create:

_____

_____

_____

_____

_____

Case study

Kathy was going for a job interview with a presentation and did this exercise. These are her lists.

<u>Good points</u>: Steady; likeable; good timekeeper; hard worker; sensible; quiet; good team player.

<u>Less good points</u>: Holds back; does not stand out; doesn't contribute to discussions; a bit stuck – does what she has always done; unconfident.

<u>The perception I would like to create</u>:
I have lots of ideas and want to share them (but sometimes need encouragement to do this); I'd like to be funny but I'm rather shy; I like variety and suggesting change; I want to be surprising.

This list enabled Kathy to see how she wanted to come over at the interview: not only as quiet and steady but also as full of ideas and someone who helped make changes. It showed her that she needed to find ways to counteract the impression that she was boring and unconfident, so she started gathering ideas from her past for her presentation, to show her initiative and dynamism. In the presentation she included some examples, to demonstrate that these positive elements were also part of her personality.

This is a reflective exercise that can be helpful when you come to do the planning and preparation for your interview presentation. You can concentrate on maximizing the beneficial perception, minimizing the less good, and adding in anything that you want to be part of the way you are perceived.

Going for a new job or a promotion is a small window of opportunity for you to reinvent yourself, especially if the panel does not know you. You can choose how to appear to them and you can reinterpret your previous experience to reflect the perception that you would like people to have of you. From the way you share examples from the past, to the way that you attack the topic of your presentation, you can influence the way you are perceived.

We have looked at what presentations in interviews are all about. You have thought about what employers are looking for and how you would like to assertively project yourself. Once you are happy with your readiness, you can move on to the next chapter to start the planning process for your knockout presentation.

Dos and don'ts

✔ Do keep trying to improve.

✔ Do reflect on what qualities you find impressive in other people you see presenting.

✔ Do keep your eyes open for hints and tips when you listen to presentations by others.

✘ Don't avoid going to interviews just because they ask you to do a presentation.

✘ Don't compare yourself to senior politicians or top-flight presenters – they have had a lifetime of practice.

✘ Don't forget that we all feel nervous under pressure. (See Chapter 4 for detailed advice on reducing feelings of nervousness).

Points to remember

1. Everyone shares similar worries about having to do a presentation.

2. No one goes in with as much confidence as they would like.

3. We can all improve.

4. Having to do a presentation gives you the chance to make the impression of your choice at your interview.

5. Everybody has their own style for projecting their image and ideas. Search for yours, find it, and use it.

Planning your presentation

In this chapter we will look at how to start planning your presentation. If you have never had to do such a thing before, it can feel like a huge mountain to climb. If we break this down into different smaller stages, the task becomes more feasible.

You need to think carefully through the planning required to fulfil a brief that you have been given. What follows explains the different kinds of subject that you may be asked to present and also how to cope with a situation where you are only told the subject of your presentation on the day, so that you have to think on your feet. At this stage we are going to concentrate on generating ideas. The next chapter will cover taking these ideas forward to use on the day of the presentation.

Presentation topics

Most presentations in an interview involve being given a question to answer or a statement to analyse. Quite often the question will be related to the job you are applying for. It may be just one aspect of the work that you are asked about or it could relate to your attitude to the job generally.

Here are some examples of the kinds of questions that can be posed as presentation subjects:

○ Why do you want this job and what would you do with it if you got it?

○ What do you see as the most important features of this job?

○ What would your priorities be in this role?

○ Outline the main factors that will lead to success in this post.

○ Prepare a five-minute outline of your ideas for developing this position.

○ What is your vision for this position?

○ What are the key issues facing this organization?

○ Explain to us in 15 minutes how you see the main strengths, weaknesses, opportunities and threats facing this company.

○ Why have you applied for this particular job?

○ What would you recommend to help us survive the next five years?

The questions can also focus on one particular, detailed area of the job:

○ Explain your strategy for growth and development.

○ Tell us in 15 minutes how you would take the IT department forward.

○ Explain how you would restructure the finance department.

○ We want to move to a more customer-focused culture. What advice would you give us?

○ Discuss the main challenges facing marketing our products.

○ Take us through your plan to increase sales for the company.

○ How would you approach formulating an efficiency plan?

○ What do you see as the role for health and safety in this engineering company?

○ In terms of public relations, outline the key audiences for this job and what you would say to them.

The question that you are set could be more about you as an individual. Here are some examples of questions that are more person-related:

○ Tell us in five minutes or less why we should employ you.

○ What experience do you bring to this job?

○ Show how you would make a mark in this company.

○ Describe your biggest work achievement and say what you learnt from it.

○ Tell us about yourself.

○ We would like to hear about your character strengths.

○ What are your main work achievements to date?

○ What is the most difficult situation you have had to deal with and what did you learn from it?

○ Tell us about some change that you have managed.

These are all presentation titles taken from real interviews. You could easily find yourself facing ones like these. The advantage of being given the topic in advance is that you can get well prepared before the day comes. Often there will be some more general instructions such as:

○ 'We would like you to present to us for no longer than 15 minutes on the following topic............ You can use any audio-visuals that you like.'

○ 'Your task is to make a presentation on the subject of............ We would like you to talk to us about this issue without any technical backup.'

○ 'Please prepare a presentation outlining the three main aspects of............ You will have 20 minutes to present your material to us. You may use projected images.'

Getting the brief on the day

Quite often you may not be told the subject of the presentation until the day of the interview itself. But never fear, normally a presentation won't just be sprung on you with no warning, you will be told in advance that the interviewers want you to come ready to put a presentation together. You will be given time to prepare – up to an hour – and materials to do it with: flip chart, PowerPoint, paper etc.

This does not mean that you need turn up on the day without anything planned. Many job applicants just relax if told that they will be given the title at the interview, give up, and think, 'Oh well, I'll just see what happens on the day then.' This is the wrong thing to do.

Quite often it is a fairly simple matter to put together a fairly accurate list of possible topics that you might be given. Indeed the secret of success when you do not know the subject of the presentation is planning around possible titles. Do not think that because you have no prior notice, you cannot know what to expect.

You need to work out what you would say for a range of possible questions so that you go to the interview as prepared as you can be. Any of the questions above could be set for you (depending on the exact job that you are applying for), so you need to have an outline plan for each of them.

Preparing for an unknown topic

The following exercise takes you through the steps.

Step 1
Start by thinking about the nature of the job for which you are applying. You can see from the lists of bullet points above that any aspect of the specific job on offer could become the topic that you will be asked to present.

Step 2
Try to create list of job aspects on which the panel might choose to ask a question. Work from the job advert, the job description, the person specification, or any information that you have been sent about the job. Underline or highlight all of the key tasks mentioned in these details, and the key features of the person required for the job. Any one of these points could be picked as the title of your presentation by the employer.

Step 3a
Take each of the underlined or highlighted tasks or job areas and really focus on it. Think of how a question on that topic could be worded. For instance, 'Experience of office management' could be turned into a question such as, 'Tell us what you see as the main skills needed for effective office management in a company like ours.'

Another such question could be, 'Tell us what you think you could bring to us in terms of office management experience.' Or the question could be worded, 'What aspects of your office management experience do you think would be relevant to our organization?'

Step 3b

Now think about the job in more general terms, and of what you would bring to it. The second set of bullet points on page 35 above looked at questions that relate to you and your application for the job. Use that list to form some questions that you could be asked.

Step 4

Now, using each of these possible questions as your starting point, under each one create three bullet points that could form the three main points of your answer. In this way you will end up with some key thoughts about how you could approach answering every question.

Here's an example:

'Tell us what you think you could bring to us in terms of office management experience.'

Key point 1 Worked in many different engineering firms, so know the sector inside out.

Key point 2 Impressive office management skills; I have run big outfits and managed staff.

Key point 3 Personality would fit in with your group; enthusiasm and motivation to succeed.

You need to create a key point list like this for each possible question that you have come up with. Then you will be prepared to take any one of them forward in the event that a similar question comes up as the title of the presentation you have to give during the actual interview.

Step 5

Work up one of these questions with your three key points into a fully planned presentation, by fleshing out the three key points. Add three things to say about each key point then think how you could introduce the topic, and add an effective conclusion to it. The more you practise turning these possible topics into full-blown presentation plans, the more confident you will feel.

What should I say in my presentation?

A big part of your planning is to decide what to say. Obviously no two presentations will be completely alike and you will create and deliver your presentation in a uniquely personal manner, but just where do you start?

To start with, turn your attention to the question you are given, but don't dash into writing things down straight away. Focus first on the subject you have been set, and think it through carefully – this is especially true if you are only set the question when you arrive at the interview. Concentrate on exactly what the question says, then work out what that means the employer wants to hear in the answer.

I have known people misinterpret the question by dashing at it and then prepare a presentation on quite the wrong subject, or at least get the emphasis wrong. Even if you come over brilliantly, if you are not answering the question properly, the panel will not be impressed.

One recruiter told me, 'We had particularly phrased the topic of the presentation to ask the candidates to deliver their speech, "as if you were talking to a group of senior managers in this organization". Not one of them obeyed that instruction. One person actually said halfway through, "Mind you, if I was addressing senior managers, I would…" – as if it were an extra part of what we had asked – when that was exactly the

entirety of what we had asked her to do! It was most exas-
perating. We did not appoint any of them for that job in the
end as none of the candidates came up to scratch.'

Thinking about the job

Planning starts with researching the correct information
about the particular vacancy you are applying for. You need
to do some detailed work before you plan your session.
Closely examine:

○ all the information you have been sent including job
description and person specification;

○ any other information on the organization, eg annual
report, the contents of their website;

○ information about similar companies by looking at
competitors' websites – collect this using a search engine
such as www.google.co.uk;

○ all you can find out about similar jobs by looking at www.
connexions-direct.com/jobs4u and other job information
sites.

Use a highlighter pen on any printed material to flag up all
the key words that you have discovered about the job, or
about the presentation topic you have been given. Now
gather your information together to give you the background
you need, to think in some depth about the presentation
topic you have been set. Do not even think of putting a presentation together without doing this research first.

One Head of Personnel said, 'We ask candidates to do a
presentation on how they see the vision for the organization
and how they can contribute to that. I find it incredible that
so many people try to make up from scratch just what our
vision should be with seemingly no information about us.
What possible use to me is that groping in the dark? What I

want them to do is find out what the vision is. If they just bothered to visit our website once, they would find that the Chief Executive writes on this very subject for anyone to read, updated every month. It is hardly rocket science but it is amazing how few people manage to check the website out before they think about what to say.'

Aids to creative thinking

Armed with all the research findings you have produced you now need to get your ideas together. Find yourself a plain piece of paper, as big as possible, turn it sideways (landscape) and write the topic of your presentation in the middle. Even better, draw a simple picture or symbol to represent the topic.

Knockout Tip!

Mapping your thoughts on the page can enhance your creativity.

Now put down all your thoughts on the page. Use pictures instead of words if you can. This kind of aid to creative thinking is sometimes called a spider diagram or spidergram. Connect up the central image or title to the first main point you think of, then draw more 'spider's legs' coming off the central point to put down your other key thoughts. Displaying your thoughts on the page in this way, so that you can see where your ideas are going, can help to release more thoughts about what to include. If you would like to learn more about spider diagrams – which are such useful thinking tools – you might like to read Tony Buzan's excellent little book on the subject, entitled *How to Mind Map* (Thorsons, London, 2002).

Examples and illustrations

For every skill you say you have, knowledge that you say you have gained, and experience that you have lived through, try to find an example or illustration of what you are saying. Just making claims about your aptitudes and abilities will not be enough. You need to find a way of 'proving' what you are saying, to make it come to life and give credibility to what you are saying.

If your topic is a presentation about yourself in some way, perhaps about how your experience fits you for the job, or what experience you have that could have taught you valuable lessons, or if your presentation is going to mention any aspect of your background, do include everything you can.

Here are some examples:

○ 'The restructuring project went well. I was told that my leadership had brought everyone together and made all the difference.'

○ 'The finances were in a mess when I arrived, but three months later we won an internal award for the way I had changed some key processes.'

○ 'Retail work is demanding but I worked as an adviser to people in the department when they needed help or guidance.'

People often feel that they should not repeat information that they have already given in the application form or CV that they submitted for the job on the basis that the panel will already have read this material. This might not be true, as the interviewing panel may not have been involved in the short-listing process. Even if they were, they will certainly not remember all the details on your form. So please do not hesitate to restate anything you need to. It is probably better when you come to do the presentation, to just start from scratch and assume they know little about you.

Be clear about your objectives

Think through what you want to achieve with your presentation. Have you been able to personally choose what to say? ('Tell us about yourself' or 'What is your greatest achievement?'). Or are you speaking to a brief set by other people ('We have a new marketing strategy, how would you implement this?'). If it is the latter, then you need to make sure that you are quite clear what the marketing strategy (in this instance) is all about. Are you clear about what they want you to do? Will they need convincing of the truth of what you are saying? If so, you may need to explain and sell an idea to them unless you know they subscribe to your views before you start.

Think through your subject

Start to jot down notes on anything that you think might be relevant to your subject-matter. Do not reject any ideas at this early stage until your plans become clearer. Allow plenty of time for this process but try not to get too bogged down in detail. You won't need to be as much of an expert as you imagine. Then, summarize exactly what you want to say into three key points.

It is always wise to avoid jargon, and sensible to use appropriate language. That way you can be sure that everyone will understand what you are talking about. If you need to include technical terms, think how you can add explanations to make it understandable to a lay person – who may also be on the panel. Exclusive language stops an audience feeling in tune with your message. Never talk down to people, and ascertain the level of expertise of the panel before you start, if that is possible.

Pitching to the audience

At this planning stage you also need to think about the audience in respect of any topics that may be current about this particular job. What issues are important to them? Is the organization going through any kind of structural change? How are they doing in the current economic climate? Are there significant competitors whom you need to mention, or not mention?

Additionally, have you been told who the individuals are on the panel? Look them up on www.google.co.uk to find out if they have some profile in the industry. Are there external experts present whom you can research for their special interests?

One woman said to me: 'I was invited onto a panel as an outside assessor by a company I was doing some research for. One bright candidate focused his presentation completely around the research project I was involved with. He must have found out that this was a big area of my work with the recruiting organization, so he knew it was bound to go down well. It may have been designed to flatter my professional interests, but it worked as far as I was concerned because he came over as canny and up-to-the-minute with his knowledge of the current state of play.'

Dealing with people you know in the audience

Having to talk to strangers is one thing but how about if you are being interviewed by a panel made up entirely of your colleagues and bosses? Most people turn into meek, unassertive wallflowers in an internal interview. They say to themselves, 'Well I have worked here for the last three years so they know who I am.'

The worst thing you can do in this situation is to assume they know all about you. I have seen it happen time and time again, when internal candidates fail to explain about their backgrounds, don't sell themselves and their expertise and do not show adequately how they would do the job. They take for granted that as they already work with these people, they hardly need to open up at all about their present role.

This is such a mistake. On the day of the interview the panel are duty-bound to pick the candidate who is the most impressive. The only way to compete and succeed is to start from scratch – as if you didn't know anyone at all. Even though you work for the organization, you need to present yourself as if you are a new face.

You must explain all about your experience, give full details of what you know and how you know those things, and prove from the outset that you would be right for the job. Forget that you have ever seen these people before and speak to them as though they are strangers. Don't assume they know or remember anything about your work history at all. After all, how much do you really know about the people you work with?

Level and style of presentation

What sort of a speech is it? A serious information briefing is quite different to a provocative, entertaining presentation. Even if it is a serious subject you may want to lighten the tone with some humour (see below). This can help to capture the attention of the audience at the start, or keep them interested later on. Can you present background information in some different way, eg handouts, slides, flip chart sheets? Too much detail in the presentation itself will not be appreciated as it will be difficult to follow.

Normally in a presentation, the panel will be looking for a certain amount of authority from your performance. The very act of taking the floor to deliver some material is fairly assertive and you need to act in that manner. What does this mean? It means being clear-sighted, businesslike, taking charge and knowing your stuff.

However, if the job is for a supervisor for a counselling service, or some other people-centred role, you want to appear accessible and friendly too. Smiling helps here, and in the next chapter we talk about facial expressions and body language. Using softer or gentler words all helps to encourage this impression.

Connecting with the audience

For an interview with a presentation you can assume that you will be presenting to a panel of at least two or three people. The presentation will go better if you can find a way of connecting with them. Can you get their views at some point, get them talking on an issue or ask them some questions? The longer the presentation, the more variety you may like to build in, rather than just be standing there talking for 20 minutes or more. Getting the panel to work together on an issue can make your presentation more memorable for them.

If you were talking about the fundraising for a charity, you could ask:

'Which is the most memorable campaign you have experienced whilst working here?' In a very short presentation, this may not be possible as you may have to concentrate on just providing them with information rather than requesting it.

One of the benefits of involving the audience is that it could mean that the attention is off you for a spell and that you are more able to get your message over. Is there anything that the audience could be involved with? Is there some activity that you could build in for variety, especially if you have a longer presentation to give? Interviews for teachers, trainers and lecturers often require a class to be taught or a lecture to be given and audience participation will be essential in such cases.

Using humour

Take a look at the material that you have put together. Is there any way that you can introduce any humorous points into what you want to say? It may be something topical, something self-deprecating about yourself, or something about the job, but a lightness of touch is always welcome.

Don't make jokes about religion, race or politics though, as you are almost bound to offend someone on the panel – which is not to be recommended. If you don't feel as if you are suited to wisecracks that is fine too. Humour is not an essential ingredient and employers are not necessarily looking for comedy in their newest member of staff.

Well done. You have worked through a planning exercise for your presentation in a thorough and methodical manner. This work will underpin your interview presentation in the same way as foundations do in any building.

If you know the precise title of your presentation you can work through the whole process before the interview day to get ready to deliver. If you do not have a title until the day itself, this planning system can be used to prepare, at a less detailed level, a number of educated guesses about the kind of subject that you will probably be given.

Let's move on now to the next chapter to see how to shape these creative thoughts into a workable structure that will prove to be a knockout at your interview.

Dos and don'ts

✔ Do leave enough time to plan your presentation properly – with or without a topic provided in advance.

✔ Do use spider diagrams to help you generate more creative ideas.

✔ Do think widely at this stage; you can cut back your material later.

✗ Don't just think 'inside the box'; this is your chance to push the boundaries back and dare to be different.

✗ Don't do too much research. The panel wants to know about your ideas, not those that you have read in an encyclopedia.

✗ Don't get panicked by the blank piece of paper in front of you; just start putting down your thoughts and they will grow.

Points to remember

1. The more you plan this out, the more confident you will get.

2. Planning helps you avoid the pitfalls that can occur on the day.

3. You wouldn't be going for this job unless you knew quite a lot about it. Have faith in your own ideas and instincts.

4. Talking through your initial ideas with a friend can help you see where you are going and give you some feedback on how it is sounding.

5. You can do just as much planning for the unseen as for the seen subject – just get your thinking cap on about possible titles and take it from there.

Preparation

In this chapter we will cover putting your presentation together. Now you have planned it all out, you are ready to get prepared. Let's think through using visual aids, the timing of your presentation and how to structure your material for the greatest impact. How to organize your notes will be considered and we will discuss rehearsing to ensure a knockout presentation.

The 10 most common mistakes

It is easy to get it wrong when designing and giving any presentation. According to employers, these are the 10 most common mistakes that people make in giving presentations during a selection process:

○ Trying to cram too much material into the time available.

○ Being too ambitious about the level of understanding of the audience.

○ Overestimating the audience's ability to take in verbal information.

○ Reading out an essay instead of a presentation.

○ Being too long-winded and using long, complicated sentences.

○ Failing to 'signpost' at any time during the speech so the audience does not know where they are or where they are going, or even when they have got there.

○ No excitement generated, no idea of passion or emotional connection.

○ Failing to 'paint pictures' by giving vivid examples.

○ Using statistics and numbers – a real killer.

○ No variation in language, voice or tempo to keep the audience awake, and use of very boring PowerPoint slides.

It will be important to keep these points in mind as we start to prepare the presentation for your interview so that we can avoid making these mistakes ourselves. Armed with what the points tell us, we can shape our original planning work into a form that can be carried through to the day of the interview itself.

Structure

You are now ready to structure your plan so that it turns into a shaped body of material, ready to deliver. Your map of your thoughts that we discussed in Chapter 2 under 'Aids to creative thinking' should have enabled you to see all the things that you could include in your presentation. Based on your thinking around the job and the research you have carried out into it, you should by now have at least one big sheet of paper full of all your creative work, brimming with ideas around some key central themes.

But how do you turn this flood of ideas and thoughts into a lucid presentation to win yourself the job? The first step is to structure what you are going to say. This will mean restricting your original page of ideas into a simple, straight-forward shape so that you can present it. You need to start by picking your three key points, to form the building blocks of your presentation.

Shaping your three key points

Knockout Tip!

Planning and structuring your presentation will make it stronger and clearer.

Warning! Do not start putting your presentation together by sitting down at the computer and writing an essay. You are going to construct your presentation out of the thinking you have already done. A strong structure for your speech comes from three main points.

Start by just looking at all the material in the spider diagram in front of you. Based on this thinking that you have already done, what would you say are the three most important points to emerge so far? Choose the three points that you think will have the most impact, make the most sense and help most to answer the question you have been set, or are planning to answer.

Group your ideas into these three clear points. Draw a ring around them or highlight them in some way. Then join up any other thoughts to these three main key points if they fit together. Now you can step back and assess this shaping work that you have just done.

If the ideas in your plan don't fit with one of your three chosen key points, they may have to be discarded. You are bound to have more material in your early planning work than you will be able to include in the final presentation.

Summarize what you want to convey, revise your plans and evaluate what you *must* include, what you *should* include and what you *could* include.

Knockout Tip!

Use this simple and straightforward structure to plan every presentation.

The 'ham sandwich'

We are going to use this shape in which to fit our presentation:

Introduction
Key point 1
Key point 2
Key point 3
Conclusion

Figure 3.1 The 'Ham Sandwich'

I call this structure the 'Rebecca Corfield Ham Sandwich'. The top box and the bottom box are the bread at either end of our sandwich. The three key points in the middle are our filling of tomato, ham and lettuce. You are now going to turn your planning sheet into material that fits neatly into these boxes above. Whatever the style, length or level of presentation you have to do, you can fit it into this structure.

Let us take a look at what goes into this structure.

What goes in the Introduction?

Your introduction is for three pieces of information to be conveyed: *who* you are, *why* you are here, *what* you intend to talk about:

1. Your name and details. (Who you are.)

2. The topic of your presentation. (Why you are here.)

3. What you are trying to achieve. (What you want to happen at the end of the presentation.)

What could the three main points be?

There are no right answers to what you should have as your three main points. You could choose three that explain:

<u>Key point 1</u> Background or context.

<u>Key point 2</u> Present situation.

<u>Key point 3</u> The future.

Examples would be included in each one to illustrate your points. Or you could choose this kind of format:

<u>Key point 1</u> What skills and experience you bring to the job.

<u>Key point 2</u> Your personality.

<u>Key point 3</u> What contribution you would make in the job.

Or, the key points could suggest three alternatives:

<u>Key point 1</u> What department A has done.

<u>Key point 2</u> What department B has done.

<u>Key point 3</u> What my department has done and why this is the best solution.

The choice of what to include depends completely on what the question asks; what your research has shown is key and how you determine to structure it. Sometimes, through your planning, you may know straight away how you want to present your material. If it is not clear immediately you may find it helpful to try out different sets of three key points until one set seems to 'fit' better than the others in the way it comes across.

Often once you move on to prepare your speech notes and rehearse, you will want to change the order of your points or make other adjustments as you start to 'hear' what you are presenting in a more immediate way.

What goes in the Conclusion?

In the conclusion you need to include a summary, action points and thanks:

1. What you said. (Remind the audience of what you have covered.)

2. Why you said it. (Explain what you were trying to achieve in your presentation.)

3. Thank you. (Thank the audience for their attention.)

You may have heard the old saying that what you want to do in a presentation is:

'Tell them what you are going to say; tell them it; and then tell them what you have told them.'

This structure above exactly represents this format. In the introduction you are telling the panel what you are going to be saying, in a micro version of the whole presentation. In the three main points you are telling them your key ideas. In the conclusion you are summarizing what it is that you have been saying.

Introduction ○ Who you are ○ Why you are here ○ What you are going to talk about
Key point 1 ○ ~~~~~~~~~~~~~~~~~~~~~~~ ○ ~~~~~~~~~~~~~~~~~~~~~~ ○ ~~~~~~~~~~~~~~~~~~~~~~
Key point 2 ○ ~~~~~~~~~~~~~~~~~~~~~~~ ○ ~~~~~~~~~~~~~~~~~~~~~~~ ○ ~~~~~~~~~~~~~~~~~~~~~~
Key point 3 ○ ~~~~~~~~~~~~~~~~~~~~~~~~ ○ ~~~~~~~~~~~~~~~~~~~~~~~ ○ ~~~~~~~~~~~~~~~~~~~~~~
Conclusion ○ What you have said ○ Why you have said it ○ Thanks

Figure 3.2 The 'Ham Sandwich'– Example

Why this structure works

Learning-theory teaches us that the attention of the audience is at its peak when we start our presentation and at the end. You know this yourself from your own experience of listening to presentations. We are alert as the speaker starts. Our attention is rapt, looking at the presenter, assessing what they look like and deciding whether they sound interesting or not.

Then, with the best will in the world and the most effort at listening, attention wanders during the middle bit. We start planning our shopping list or thinking about work or just day-dreaming. But as soon as the speaker says, 'So, to summarize what I have been saying...' our attention snaps back to them again.

Advantages of Introduction and Conclusion

By having an introduction and conclusion that both summarize your key points, you are effectively giving your audience three blasts of your message and making the most of the times when they are naturally most attentive – at the beginning and the end. Even if members of the panel drift off slightly as you cover your main three points in the body of your presentation, they will have had the summary in the introduction and get it again in the conclusion. You stand more chance of being understood, being attended to and, most importantly, of being remembered.

Conversely, if you just dive straight in to your material, rush through it and then stop abruptly at the end, your audience will probably follow what you are saying for the first third and the last third of your material but may well find their minds wandering during the middle part. This is not much help if you want them to make any sense of what you are presenting to them. That is why the introduction and conclusion are so important.

Make sure you introduce yourself and your subject properly in every presentation, even when you think that people know who you are and why you are there. Try to end on an upbeat note and include personal examples where possible.

Using humour

If you have planned to be funny, you need to signpost this clearly to the audience. When you listen to established comics they tell you when you are expected to laugh: 'I'll tell you a funny story...', 'That reminds me of a joke I heard...', 'You'll laugh at this...', 'Here's an amusing example of what I have been saying...', so that we are primed to be listening out for a joke and are ready to laugh at it.

Here are the most common unfunny mistakes:

○ Trying to be wacky and eccentric to stand out from the crowd.
  There is funny ha-ha and funny peculiar. The first might enliven your presentation, the latter definitely will not. A job interview is rarely the place to appear very different. Even if an employer wants a risk-taker, they will shy away from someone who comes across as plain peculiar. Keep your dramatic and crazy ideas for once you have got the job. Don't risk putting the panel off you by being too weird.

○ Not signposting (see below) that a joke is coming – just diving straight in to it.
  Give the audience a chance to laugh at your funny points. Tell them that you have got something that they will find

funny and the chances are they will. If you just launch into an amusing comment, the probability is it will be missed.

○ Not leaving long enough after the joke for the audience to get it and laugh at it.
And if you do tell a joke don't rush on afterwards in an embarrassed way. Pause, let the punch line sink in, then you will reap the reward.

○ Being put off and demoralized when the audience doesn't laugh or get the joke.
Even the funniest comic doesn't score a hit with every line. Don't give up if you don't score a bullseye with every attempt. It won't ruin your presentation if they don't fall about laughing. Make a note afterwards about what worked and what didn't. If you ever have to give such a presentation again you can adjust things then.

○ Getting confused and flustered when the audience starts laughing a couple of seconds later.
If you rush on past a joke, it can prove funny a couple of minutes later when people have had time to assimilate what has been said. There will be confusing laughter that does not seem to tally with any funny comment.

○ Rushing on to the next thing before the laughter has finished.
If you got a laugh, let it finish properly before you move on. People like the chance to smile or giggle if they find you amusing, and you don't want them to miss your next point by moving on too fast.

○ Not milking the goodwill after the joke.
If it worked, perhaps you can make more of the point.

Feedback

Now you have written what you think will work as a presentation, talk it through with someone to see what feedback you get. Ask the person to tell you what you were talking about and see if they can offer feedback on what went well and what could be improved. Don't ask for feedback about what they didn't like though. Unless it can be phrased in terms of a positive suggestion, we don't want it.

Prompt cards

Now you are ready to mould your presentation into a form from which you can deliver it. You do not want to turn up on the interview day with a pile of closely typed A4 sheets of paper that you plan to read out. For a start, paper shakes and rustles if you have hands that are trembling through nerves, and a heap of paper will only make the panel think that you are going to go well over your allotted time.

You will have more impact if you can just work from cards that have your key points on them. Index cards can be bought at big stationers and they come in different sizes and colours. I recommend A5 size plain, unlined white cards. You can always cut up your own from A4 card if you have difficulty finding them.

Cards give the impression that you only need the minimum of prompting, can be kept easily and just slipped into a pocket, and because they are smaller than A4 paper, mean that you will not be able to write down every word that you plan to say. In this way they become real prompt cards, just with words to cue you in to your next key point but not a full script safety net.

Connecting with the audience

Think of all the speakers you have listened to, the conferences you have attended, the presenters you have seen. The
people who most get to you don't sit with their heads buried
in a script or a book as they speak. That is why leading politicians use the autocue, so that they can have the words in
front of them but still give the impression of looking at the
audience. We need a way to have a reminder of what we
want to say but we also need to have a direct connection with
our audience. This is particularly true at a presentation in an
interview, when we need to convince them to employ us.

Your impact with your audience increases proportionately
with the amount of time you manage to have eye contact
with the people you are talking to. Read every word from the
printed page and the panel will feel quite distanced from you.
Look often at your audience and they will feel you are talking
directly to them and they will attend and remember much
more.

Flexibility and impact

Prompt cards do not provide you with a total script, just a
guide to the key points you want to convey, leaving you with
a certain amount of flexibility in the way you choose to do
this. This is what helps with impact though, as you will
sound much more immediate and conversational than if you
were reading out every single word.

Be aware that the words you use will form part of the
impression you create. Mild terms and gentle adjectives will
create a picture of someone safe and mainstream. Strong
descriptors and tough phrases will indicate a robust
attitude.

Note the difference in these pairs of phrases:

'I believe it to be true.'

'I am absolutely convinced of it.'

'On the whole this is the way it happens.'

'Every single time we see this happen.'

'I think we should…'

'I am determined that our best plan is…'

'I am fairly sure about this.'

'It is completely obvious.'

Signposts

When you write your notes, add in 'signposts'. This means telling the audience where you have got to in the presentation and where you are going next:

'I would like to introduce this presentation…'

'So here is my first key point: the background to this situation…'

'Now I am going to move on to the second point I want to make…'

'And my final point is about the way forward for this department…'

'So those were my three main points.'

'To conclude my presentation…'

If you make it crystal clear exactly where you have got to in your presentation, the panel will find it easier to follow you, get your meaning, and appreciate the points you are making – which is surely the object of the exercise.

Prompt cards: Summary

○ Use coloured and highlighter pens.

○ Use one card for each of your three key points and one for the Introduction and the Conclusion.

○ Just write down points you want to mention in note form on each card.

○ Include examples to illustrate each point you make.

○ Use positive, strong words to express what you want to say.

○ Don't forget to add 'signposts' to show where you are in the presentation.

○ Add stage instructions to yourself such as 'Pause here' and 'Smile!'

○ Punch a hole and use a treasury tag to tie the cards together.

○ Number your cards in case you get lost.

○ Keep the cards afterwards as a record of your presentation.

Using visual aids and props

You may be offered all kinds of computer facilities, flip charts or other visual aids to use in doing your presentation. Think this through carefully. Just because something is offered, you don't necessarily have to take up that option. If you have not planned to illustrate your presentation with some kind of visual display it might be better to avoid using anything. Unless you know you are dealing with a large audience or need to put across particularly complex material, it will normally do you no favours to use it.

The exceptions could be:

○ needing photographs or other illustrations;

○ diagrams that cannot easily be explained;

○ requiring charts or graphs to illustrate figures or statistics.

Format

Even if you are well used to using PowerPoint, in a short presentation a simple handout of your main points – preferably with some sort of visual image – will be ample. When you are under stress anyway, it is not the best time to get caught up with electronic equipment and technical processes unless it is vital that you do so. Most people use a visual display merely to duplicate everything that they are saying anyway – which is guaranteed to bore the audience. Use diagrams and pictures rather than quote statistics or figures. If clearly displayed, charts and graphs can be useful, but a lasting paper handout may have a lot more impact.

Keep your graphic images simple though, and try to ensure that they add something to what you are saying. Let your message do the talking, not the technology.

A human resources manager said: 'Everyone has to do a presentation. They all troop in with their PowerPoint slides ready and my heart sinks. The slides are inevitably just the same as the words they have just told us, just repetition of what the person is saying. Why do people keep doing this? It is just daft and there's nothing more likely to switch me off from selecting those people. The one who just talks engagingly to me is normally the hands-down winner.'

PowerPoint is, however, a useful tool, and may be used in appropriate situations.

Using PowerPoint

PowerPoint can help you create any kind of display that you want. If you do decide to use it for your presentation you may find the following tips helpful:

- ○ The PowerPoint program is very user-friendly. Take a look at it if you have not used it before. Explore all the different types of visual aid that it offers. The AutoContent wizard gives you hints and tips for starting to explore what can be done and is a good place to begin playing around.

- ○ PowerPoint offers you many pre-prepared presentations into which you can slot your own words or images. Although these may be helpful for some occasions, generally you will find it more flexible to create your own blank presentation and then use the set layouts it has.

- ○ Learn how to promote and demote text (make it bigger or smaller) to add emphasis by pressing a button. Don't copy book pages or type unless you enlarge the print first – check this from the back of the room when you rehearse. There is nothing worse than tiny illegible words on the screen.

- ○ When preparing slides for projecting onto a screen, pick a dark colour for the text. Light bright colours don't show up well for text but you can use them for highlighting titles, bullet points or key points.

- ○ There are an astonishing number of images available on the internet which include pictures, cartoons and symbols. Look at Clip Art on your computer – copyright-free images that you can use as you like in any presentation. You can also buy CDs full of thousands more images commercially.

○ Use landscape rather than portrait format. Remember the '6, 7, 8' rule: keep to a maximum of 6 words per line; 7 lines per page; using letters at least 8 mm high (point size 28). Leave a 2 cm margin around the edge always.

○ Do not use words when you could use a picture and do not present data as raw numbers; use pie charts, graphs or any other visual image to demonstrate relationships. Do not put more than one idea on each screen.

○ Try to avoid turning your back on the interview panel members, and pointing, and looking, only at the screen. Keep addressing the audience, and do not block their view of the screen, making sure it is clear even from the back of the room. Stop talking each time you change to a new screen, and if you stop referring to it, switch the computer off.

A very useful book if you want more comprehensive help is: *The PowerPoint Detox* by Patrick Forsyth. You can find full details in 'Further reading from Kogan Page' at the end of this book.

Technology

Gremlins can attack the technology that you have planned to use, at any time. If you have vital visual aids to accompany your presentation, you must make sure that you have a back-up. Take a spare copy along in case you cannot make yours work on the day. The computer technology may also totally fail to function, so you should also prepare some alternative, or at least be able to give your presentation without the primary visual back-up you had planned.

I recently saw an example of someone who found they could not use the computer presentation they had prepared. They gave the presentation orally and managed perfectly well because they had rehearsed doing it this way just in case the computer did not work. The moral here is: prepare what you know you can control and expect the worst from what you cannot.

Using flip charts

If you decide to go 'low-tech' (and sometimes you are requested not to use any electronic equipment in your presentation), you may decide to use a flip chart. If this is the case, there are some rules that you can use to ensure that you make the best use of this tried and trusted visual aid:

○ Write a maximum of eight words per line, keep to eight lines per page at the most, use note form only.

○ Use squared flip chart paper to help with layout if you are drawing anything.

○ Make sure you have enough sheets and spare pens always.

○ If you prepare your sheets in advance, make sure you have a neat and effective way of fixing them to the board.

○ Write in print, using larger letters than you think you need.

○ Pencil lines on the chart beforehand, to keep your writing straight.

○ Whenever possible use different bold colours, pictures and images.

○ Draw diagrams in fine pencil in advance, then ink them over on the day.

○ Use tabs with labels, if you need to find a page quickly on the pad.

○ Always stop talking when you are writing.

○ Turn the page over when you have finished referring to it.

Audience participation

If you have planned to involve the audience in some way in your presentation, you now need to prepare any materials that you need. If they are to be asked questions, given a form to fill in or will be working in small groups, you need to get all your physical resources ready before the event. Will you need a handout to give out at the end? If so, make sure it looks good, that you have enough copies and that your name is clearly laid out on it.

Rehearsing

No actor goes on stage without proper rehearsals – the final one in full dress. Spend time rehearsing the material to generate your own enthusiasm and confidence about what you are going to say. No actor would feel even half-ready for the opening night without practising fully to help learn their words, and to build up expertise about, and experience of, what the role entails.

Do not be tempted to add more material each time you rehearse – a simple message is more likely to have the impact you intend. However, you sometimes discover at this stage that you want to alter the shape of what you have prepared. You may find that in reading out your material, it does not quite hang together or have the impact that you imagined. It is fine to tweak the order of your points at this stage; indeed, this aspect of your preparation is vital, to act as a last check on what you have planned to say.

Once you are sure that the three main points that you have designed make sense and have impact, have confidence in them and stick to them. It does not matter if you go off a point slightly in the rehearsal, as long as you adhere to your overall plan. After all, nobody knows exactly what is on your prompt cards except you: the whole beauty of them is that they do not tell you every word to speak; you are reminded of the point you wish to make, but you are retaining a freshness in your words by being able to slightly alter them at every run through.

Reconnaissance

Take the idea of rehearsing to every aspect of the interview. Can you visit the premises for a dummy run prior to the event? It can be very helpful to know where the main entrance is located, the time it will take to get to the venue and how difficult it is to park nearby or to get to the location from the station or bus stop. Think through any questions you want to ask the panel and also any questions that they may want to ask you. If you can be prepared on these points it will help you answer confidently on the day.

Timing

Rehearse too using a stopwatch. Speaking your words out loud makes a big difference to the length of time you think your presentation may take compared to when you just read it through in your head. You must ensure that you stick to the time limit that you have been set. You may well just be cut off by the panel if you go over the time. If this happens it can shake your nerve and wreck the presentation entirely.

Many presentations go on too long. A presentation may have sounded fine in practice but when they go live, some people waffle, go off the point and lose valuable time. Before you know it, the time has gone and you have been stopped in your tracks – it can be even worse if you overshoot but no one stops you.

One Senior HR manager tells us: 'When you are in a hole, stop digging. We had a candidate recently who had been set a time limit of six minutes for his presentation. He carried on until nine minutes was up and then said, "Oh, this isn't going very well is it?", and then proceeded to continue on for another six minutes. By the end he had used up 15 minutes in total and made himself look as if he was completely unable to follow instructions. At the very least he could have called it short at nine minutes, once he first realized that he had gone way over the time allocated, but no, he made it all much worse by carrying on regardless.'

Work out the timing of each section of the structure and keep a close eye on the time as you practise speaking; plan for misjudging it, and build in a couple of extra points that you can use if the time is available. Talking into a tape recorder is a good way of timing what you will say.

Preparing for questions

Most presentations are open to questions from the panel afterwards. You may well find that you are asked for more details on some of the points you present, or are questioned on some aspect of your material. These questions need not take you by surprise, if you think through at this preparation stage, all the possible topics of interest.

Imagine you have never heard your presentation before; what might remain unclear? Think through each of your key points; would there be an obvious question to ask about them? When you rehearse in front of people (see Chapter 4), ask them if any questions occur to them when you have finished. You can even be asked about the way that you put your presentation together, so don't assume that all questions will relate only to the content of your speech; they may also range more widely and may cover your experience of constructing your presentation.

By now you should feel keen to present your material. You have prepared it fully – to sound just the way you want – from structuring your words, to arranging your prompt notes, to rehearsing. You are ready to move on, and the next chapter tells you more about delivering a knockout presentation.

Dos and don'ts

✔ Do produce a handout for the panel with your key points, a visual, and your name on it if this is helpful.

✔ Do discipline yourself to stick to your three main points that you planned.

✔ Do avoid jargon and exclusive technical or specialist language.

✗ Don't pitch what you are saying too high – there may be people there who are not following you.

✗ Don't try to cram too much into the time. Less can be more.

✗ Don't talk in a different style to normal conversation except to make it bigger, bolder and more definite.

Points to remember

1. Effective presentations need thorough preparation.

2. Structuring your presentation is the most helpful thing to do to add impact.

3. Visual aids can help to tell your story.

4. Rehearsing what you have planned to do will improve your confidence on the day.

5. Try to think through every aspect of your presentation.

Presentation

This chapter is concerned with conveying your material to your audience, the panel, as part of your interview. You have fully planned your presentation as far as you can, and have taken intelligent guesses if you have not been given the title yet. You have organized your preparation in all its aspects including getting ready for the questions you may be asked. As far as you can be, you are on top of your material. Now you need to think through the aspects of speaking your material out loud.

Here we look at all aspects of delivering your presentation – the most daunting part. It is fine to sit and mull over your ideas but the day is coming nearer when you will be expected to stand up in front of that panel and deliver the goods. We will consider all aspects of your physical presence and image, and what affects how confident you look and feel. Facial expression and body language are as much part of giving a presentation as what you are going to say.

Handling nerves is difficult but can be done.

Your personal image

Before you go to an interview it is worth thinking about your personal image, how you come across to other people, and –

perhaps more importantly – how you would like to come across to your interview panel. When doing a presentation, *you* are in control of what you say, the way you are saying it and how you look, so you can design the impression that you want to convey to some extent.

We are all highly influenced by the way people look. We receive messages of suitability and competence from the visual images portrayed by other people. This is even more true in an interview situation where the panel is looking for evidence on which to judge you.

Obviously you cannot change the way you look to any large extent but you can rethink your image in the details. Although marginal changes and improvements won't get you a job on their own, if you are one of two candidates who are both suitable, it could be your general look and demeanour that mean you get chosen for the job.

Authority

There are slightly different issues for men and women when it comes to appearance and image. Women are faced with many more fashion and style messages which only serve to confuse. Your job interview is not the place to try to be a fashion icon or style leader. Your presentation will benefit if you look businesslike (whether the job is in business or not) and restrained.

Dress

For instant impact, dress one level more smartly than usual. A jacket is essential for a short presentation to a large audience where you need to grab their attention straight away. For women my advice is to confine your clothing choices to a plain suit or jacket and skirt/trousers in a dark colour. Navy blue and mid-grey suit everybody. Contrast this with a light plain blouse or top under the jacket for authority.

There is a danger that panels can assume that the female candidates for a job won't be as tough or robust as the male competition. Don't let that assumption be held against you. Doing your presentation is not the time to be looking at your most feminine and gorgeous. Save that for when you are celebrating afterwards.

Some style points for women:

○ Dress soberly. Always go for a neutral look. Avoid low-cut tops, figure-hugging clothes and short skirts totally.

○ Make sure that you are able to stand and walk easily in the shoes you wear and don't have the heels too high.

○ Tie your hair back if it is long and swishy and particularly if you are apt to keep fiddling with it or pushing it out of your eyes.

○ Reduce the accessories and jewellery you use to a minimum and keep them classic and simple. Just have one work bag with you if you need one. If you must have a handbag, keep that inside the work bag.

And for men:

○ Wear a darker suit and a white (but not too bright white) shirt.

○ Do wear a tie, even if you wouldn't often wear one in the job if you get it. It remains an indicator of having made an effort and implies you are trying to look smart.

○ Have clean hair, smart proper shoes (polished), and do your jacket up when you are standing up.

○ Wear plain socks that match – or are darker – than your trousers, and long enough that you don't reveal bare calves if you cross your legs.

Don't be tempted to wear something wacky or surprising to your interview. Leave the novelty tie or vividly-coloured socks at home until you get the job. Looking different is not the priority. You may be remembered for it, but not in the right way. Panels on the whole would rather employ people with a businesslike appearance than for their individual style or clothing sense. Never wear anything distracting which will divert attention from your message – plain colours are best: you want the audience to focus on the message not on the messenger.

Handling nerves

You may be surprised to read this, but even the most experienced speaker needs to get nervous in order to perform well. To understand this we need to first explain what creates such initial feelings of nervousness.

Understanding nerves

What are nerves? Nerves are actually the manifestation of the release of adrenalin into the system. Adrenalin is a hormone that is released when we face perceived danger and we feel its effects when we are scared or threatened in some way. It is part of our bodily defence system when under attack. This 'fight or flight response' concentrates oxygen where it will be most useful for the very physical response of fighting our way out of trouble or running away.

This means that our muscles in our arms and legs are powered up, but that oxygen is drained from those areas that will not be needed, ie the brain, fingers, toes, hands and feet. The digestive system temporarily shuts down.

Other quite normal and frequently experienced symptoms include:

○ dry mouth;

○ loss of hearing;

○ loss of peripheral vision;

○ rapid heartbeat and accelerated breathing rate;

○ paling or flushing, or alternating between both;

○ churning stomach and feeling of nausea;

○ the urge to visit the toilet together with an inability to actually go to the toilet.

These responses are a throwback to our ancestors, who had little choice about their reactions when they regularly faced dangerous situations. Whilst this automatic chain of events was no doubt very helpful if you needed to run away or fight the enemy in prehistoric times, it is not very productive when we have to give any kind of presentation in the modern world.

Most of all in the interview, you need your brain: to listen to the audience; to gauge their responses; to see what is happening; to speak clearly and to react swiftly. Finding it short of oxygen and almost closing down represents a disaster. Nerves will affect everyone too. They are no respecters of maturity or confidence. However, do not give up just yet. There are ways of beating your feelings of nervousness.

Methods of control

There are a couple of nerve control methods that are very effective.

1. This is a useful little exercise to do before you start your presentation:
If you can, find a place to be alone, and slowly say the vowel sounds 'A – E – I – O – U', making your mouth stretch as

much as possible whilst speaking each letter in turn. This limbers up the muscles around the mouth, which will enable you to speak as you have planned and to enunciate clearly.

This is such a useful exercise to do. If you can't speak the words, just stretch your mouth around the sounds and say them silently. I always do this before any public appearance as a warm-up before speaking – often as I walk down a corridor on the way in to the event.

You may not want to do it out loud in front of all the other interview candidates as you may look slightly alarming. Or perhaps you would, as a way to totally unnerve them all, seeing you pulling peculiar faces and snarling silently to yourself.

Knockout Tip!

A little deep breathing will counteract the worst physical symptoms of nerves.

2. Here is a highly effective breathing exercise which will help to keep you calm and which can rescue you if you go blank:

The main effect of adrenalin is to reduce the amount of oxygen in the bloodstream. To counter this we need to take in more breath – not in a panicky or evident way, but calmly and in a controlled manner.

Take a few deep breaths before entering the room or just before you begin, and rest your hands on a lectern or table if one is available. Have a glass of water near in case your mouth becomes dry. If you start to go blank in the middle of your presentation, pause in your material and simply take some deep breaths. Sure enough your mind will clear and you will be able to continue.

When nerves hit in any stressful situation: stop, breathe deeply and wait. It is the antidote to the fight or flight response.

Projecting yourself

Delivering a presentation requires you to project yourself – make yourself seem bigger, louder, altogether larger than life in order to make the impression you need. Think about how you would do presentations if you got the job and you had to give presentations like this as part of your day job. If you envisage yourself actually doing the job you will find that this helps you to put yourself forward assertively.

If you have worries about something, expressing it to the audience often helps. For instance, if you have a sore throat on the day or have any worries about the visual aids you are using, a short sentence to alert people to the fact may help you put it to one side during the presentation. Worrying about something that you also feel you have to hide just adds to the pressure and feels intimidating.

Voice

Add variety to your tone to keep the audience alert. Do not rush your words – most people speak too fast under pressure. Practise speaking higher and lower and observe the effects. You need to speak with more variety than usual because, to some extent, you are performing. You are trying to project yourself as slightly bigger, bolder and brighter than normal when, typically, you are just talking across a table in a meeting. Holding the floor necessitates grabbing and holding the attention of your audience, and you need to perform in order to achieve that.

But do not try to put on a fancy voice or a different way of speaking. Use the same voice and language that you use to talk to people every day, but project to the back of the room and try to make the volume of your voice louder and include more variety of tone to add drama and interest.

If you feel you need more practice at this, find a large room and get a friend to stand at the far end. Practise speaking loudly enough for them to hear you easily, and remember what increase in volume you need in order to achieve this.

Accent

Some people worry that their accent will be held against them by the panel if they sound different. Our accents are very difficult to change and the variety of accents add to the richness of our culture. If you know you have a strong accent, just make an effort to speak more slowly to ensure people listening can follow you. But overall, feel proud of the way you speak and your confidence will be transmitted.

Pauses

Pauses can be very powerful as they add emphasis to your speech and allow you time to collect your thoughts while the audience is catching up with what you have just said. Pausing in your speech feels terrible. Most people think that if they pause, it sounds as if they have forgotten their words. However, most pauses do not sound nearly as endless to the audience as they do to you.

We worry that the audience will think we have dried up completely. In fact a pause or two seems fine to the audience and never seems to last as long as it does to the speaker. Pauses will allow the audience to catch up with what they have heard so far, and therefore often do them a favour. They can also be a chance for you to collect your thoughts, take a deep breath and regain control, so always build some into your presentation.

Facial expression
Smiling

The most important facial expression is smiling. Always smile when you greet and leave your audience. It makes you look confident and as though you want to be there. It is the way we signify being relaxed and connected to other people.

Good first impressions are created mainly by the way you appear to others, and a pleasant look on your face helps with this. As the speaker you want to be noticed and to hold the audience's attention without looking odd. Smiling also counteracts our natural expression when we are concentrating on remembering what we are going to say – which is frowning.

To check out the beneficial effect of smiling, try doing it on the bus or in the supermarket checkout queue. You will find people smiling back at you almost automatically. This sets up a happy circle of reassurance and reinforcement that will help you no end as you start your presentation. It feels much better to be faced with gently smiling faces on your panel than ones staring blankly back at you.

Eye contact

In the audience, if we think a speaker is looking at us, it gives us the impression that we are being directly addressed. This helps us to attend and focus on what the person is saying to us. Your aim is to try to engage the whole audience, so you need to keep your eyes moving around to give them all the same impression.

Some interview presentations can be to a larger audience. For instance, with an interview for a lecturing, training or teaching position, you may well have to give a sample class or lecture. With a large audience you will not be able to catch everybody's eye, but remember to glance around the room when you can. Following an 'M' or 'W' shape with your eyes in a large area allows you to cover the space and gives the impression that you are relating to everyone.

Body language

The way we move and the way we stand and gesticulate reveal a lot about our innermost feelings. If we appear confident on the outside, the audience will think we are feeling that way, so good body language can help you win the battle over looking nervous.

Be aware that folded arms, crossed legs and hunched shoulders can give a slight impression of defensiveness, particularly if they are all seen together. Most of us tend to adopt this body language unconsciously when under pressure. Make a big effort to stop yourself so that you endorse the impression that you are happy and relaxed.

Nervous habits

Hands in your pockets jingling coins and other repetitive gestures such as endlessly flicking hair back are signs of nerves and can be distracting. When you rehearse your presentation, watch yourself in a mirror to check that you perform and make your message clear, without being too over-the-top.

If you think you will need some reminders to nudge you out of habitual behaviour, use your prompt cards to write messages to yourself such as 'hands out of pockets' or 'keep still' or 'leave the hair alone', to remind yourself to be stable and stationary as far as possible.

If your natural style is to use gestures, then just act as normal. There is nothing wrong with moving your hands around to make a point, and we use gestures to aid understanding. Just be careful that you are not over-reacting and looking jumpy. Try to read more about the fascinating subject of body language, and make it work so you deliver your message with impact.

Sit or stand?

If you get the choice of sitting or standing and the room you are in is big enough – stand up. This gives you more confidence and ensures that you can be seen. Obviously if there is only one person interviewing you, then it might appear slightly over the top to stand up and tower over them, but if you have a panel of two or more, it could well be to your advantage to stand up. For a start, it enables you to move, speak, breathe and perform properly, with opened up lungs and wide shoulders. It also looks less meek and mild.

Stance

Face your audience squarely, use all the space available to you and stand as tall as you can. Stand with both feet flat on the floor to ensure that you do not start to do a little dance out of nervous excitement – when under pressure, that nervous energy often finds odd places to exhibit itself. If you are not standing solidly, you may well find your feet tapping and moving repetitively, out of your control. Your feet should be shoulder-width apart, and you should resist the temptation to cross your legs one in front of the other – you could fall over.

I once heard of a candidate in laced knee-high boots who stood with her legs crossed quite comfortably to give her presentation. To her horror she found that the hooks of one boot had become entangled with the laces of the other boot and she simply could not disentangle them to walk back to her seat at the end of her presentation. She had an awkward few moments of being bent double, with her head between her knees, scrabbling around behind her before she could disentangle the boots from one another. This is not really a cool look at an important interview presentation.

Coping with distractions

If something untoward happens in your presentation, you need to keep calm. More importantly – you need to keep going. Always expect the unexpected. Someone may walk into the room uninvited; a display may crash down from the wall; your laptop may stop working; you may have a coughing fit in the middle of the presentation. You still need to retain your aplomb and finish the presentation as and when you can. Things can often go wrong, but what counts in the minds of the audience is the way that you handle it – don't let it stop you in your tracks.

Staying confident

Overall, a few slips in your delivery won't lose you the job. At a recent interview where I sat on a panel as an external assessor, a very nervous candidate fluffed parts of his presentation, but ended up getting the job. It was clear that he was the best candidate, despite his nerves. The quality of what he was saying reached out beyond his nervous demeanour to show us that he was the right candidate to choose.

We have considered aspects of delivering your presentation from handling nerves to deciding what to wear. Now you have worked through all the hints and tips in this book you are almost ready to give your presentation in your interview. It will be a knockout. The next chapter covers the kinds of queries you may have left and looks at some common myths about presentations. You are nearly ready to go with your presentation.

Dos and don'ts

✔ Do enjoy making your presentation. It is a privilege to be able to give your views in this way.

✔ Do stay focused on the things you want to say. This will carry you through.

✔ Do get over your feelings of self-consciousness and shyness. The panel needs to hear your message.

✗ Don't forget that you have been shortlisted to be at this interview – you have won through to this stage so far and you are doing well.

✗ Don't get bogged down with too much detail – make sure the key points come across.

✗ Don't try so hard to be perfect in every respect that you constrain yourself. Act naturally and perform for the panel.

Points to remember

1. Even a very nervous candidate can come through as the winner.

2. Breathe deeply if you find everything is falling apart (and even if you don't).

3. Smile – at the start and the end of your presentation at least.

4. Project yourself – act bigger, stronger, more definite than you feel.

5. Express your worries and get rid of them.

Learning and improving

This chapter covers how to increase your learning and improve the way you make a presentation during a job interview. Presentation skills are something on which you can build. The better you get, the more confident you will find you are in all areas of your life.

If presentation skills will be integral in your life – as part of your job and future prospects – then you may appreciate some tips for moving on in your speaking career. This could involve using the same skills, speaking to bigger audiences and work conferences, and participating more in meetings, seminars etc. You may also consider using your skills to take the chair in meetings. All these topics are covered in this chapter.

You can evaluate your presentations in a variety of ways so that you build learning into your experience over time. We look at how to get feedback on your style to monitor the quality of your presentations, as well as how you can do the same for friends and colleagues. No one is an expert right from the word go and the more chances you get to build on your experience at giving presentations, the better you will do each time you are set one as part of an interview.

Self-evaluation

But at any stage, how can you tell how you are doing? One way is to reflect on experiences and come to your own conclusions about how they went.

Each time you have an interview, as soon as you leave the interview room, write down all the thoughts you have about how you did in your presentation, and any questions that you were asked. Put down as accurately as you can remember, what you answered to each one too. You will be surprised at how quickly your memory fades about details such as these, and so what you can recall can prove incredibly useful for the future, especially if you intend going for similar jobs again.

Knockout Tip!

Reflecting on past experiences can be a powerful tool for improving your performance.

The following checklist might be useful as a prompt:

Checklist
Who was on your panel; what job positions did they hold?

_____

_____

_____

Think through how you felt as the presentation was going along.

_____

_____

_____

Did any parts go better or worse than you expected?

_____

_____

_____

By the end of it, how do you feel it went?

_____

_____

_____

How did the panel seem to react as it progressed?

_____

_____

_____

How would you change or improve it for the next time?

_____

_____

_____

Write down the questions the panel asked you about your presentation...

_____

_____

_____

_____

_____

_____

...and how you answered each one:

_____

_____

_____

_____

_____

_____

_____

On reflection, how could you have improved any of your answers?

_____

_____

_____

How do you think the questioning part went overall?

_____

_____

Do you have any other reflections on your presentation as a whole?

_____

_____

_____

Is there any action that you will take as a result of this experience?

_____

_____

_____

Complete this checklist every time you do a presentation in an interview – as soon as possible afterwards – and file the results in your job applications file. If you haven't got one of these, get a smart, new file in which to keep all your job-related paperwork. It can save you lots of time when you are preparing for an interview, if you don't have to start from scratch again. It should also provide you with reminders of the key learning points from your presentation experiences.

Getting feedback

Self-evaluation, however, is just your own view of what happened. It can be very difficult to get an objective picture of your overall performance after the interview is over. We don't really know how we truly performed in the interview presentation – only the members on your panel do. They are the only ones who have seen your performance compared to those of the other candidates. They have contrasted your work with other people's. Therefore it makes sense to ask the employer how you have done after the event.

Most employers will be pleased to give you feedback on your performance as long as you ask them nicely. But be warned, if you ask in a grumpy manner or seem threatening, they could well think that you are trying to collect evidence in order to take out a grievance against them for not giving you the job.

Here are some examples of what NOT to say:

'I obviously haven't got the job – the least you can do is tell me what your reasons were.'

'I want to know why you thought I wasn't good enough to do the job.'

'You decided to give the job to someone else and I want to know why.'

'Now you have to justify making that bad decision.'

Ringing up to get feedback is best done by asking politely if they can give you any tips on your performance.

Knockout Tip!

Finding out how others perceive you can provide a useful, different perspective.

Here are some approaches to try:

'I would be grateful for any feedback you could give me.'

'This is the kind of job I am really keen to get. Can you give me any comments about how I came over?'

'If you could give me any guidance or tips on how I can improve, it would help me a lot.'

'I enjoyed the interview and even though I wasn't successful, I know I can learn from your feedback.'

Be ready with a pen and paper to take notes on what you are told. Don't give your opinion on what you hear or challenge anything; it is too late to change the result now, and you may only put them off telling you all they could. Just note each point down, ask further questions if any of their comments are unclear, and thank them at the end for their time.

Good feedback will tell you what you did well at, as well as telling you what you could improve.

Make your lists look like this:

Things they said I did well   Things they said I could improve

_____   _____

_____   _____

_____   _____

_____   _____

Then underneath write yourself another list.

The ways I can improve are:

_____

_____

_____

In this section you could put any suggestions that are practical ways of improving your chances of success next time round.

Case study

Here are lists written by a candidate called James:

Things they said I did well   Things they said I could improve

○ Confident approach   ○ Wider understanding of the industry

○ Clear speaking voice   ○ More variety in the presentation

○ Presentation well planned   ○ Could look smarter

Some ways I can improve are:

○ Attend more conferences; read professional journal regularly.

○ Practise more exciting deliveries in work presentations.

○ Buy a new interview suit.

James was happy that the feedback from the employer had given him some areas to work on that could not fail to help his chances the next time around.

Biting the bullet

It is not always easy to find out what you have done wrong and I have known many people who never asked for feedback for various reasons:

'They never tell you the truth anyway, they just want to fob you off.'

'They probably only appointed the favourite internal candidate and the whole thing was just staged for equal opportunities reasons.'

'I didn't get the job, that's bad enough. Why would I want to make it all worse by them telling me why I failed?'

'I just want to forget the whole horrible episode now and move on.'

Although it can be hard to hear about the areas in which you under-performed, it is worth trying to get feedback in case you find out information to your advantage. It can often turn out that the reasons you thought you lost the job were not actually the main reasons for your not being offered it.

Case study

Chris, a candidate for a teaching job, said, 'Oh I know exactly why I didn't get the job. They asked me a question about my passions at work and that was what lost it for me. I'd already said that I was very interested in using my musical skills in the job and so I did not know what to say to this question in order to offer them anything else. I hardly answered that question at all and I could see the goodwill of the panel just ebbing away.'

In fact the panel found the answer Chris gave to that particular question to be perfectly satisfactory. It was actually his presentation that let him down. His content was shallow and his answers were just less deep than those of the other candidates. He seemed not to have realized that he would be asked some quite probing questions. The interview finished quite early as, overall, his answers were so short compared to those of the other candidates.

After receiving this information at feedback Chris was able to see his entire interview performance in more perspective. Being so concerned about a single question that perplexed him – and his answer to it – he would never have realized that it was in his presentation he had lost the interview, and that his lack of success was nothing to do with any one individual answer. He was now able to think anew about what he should put into a similar presentation for his next interview to improve his prospects.

In my experience, most employers are happy to give you feedback, and some can be impressed by you seeking it out.

Case study

Sonia was turned down for a job but rang to get feedback anyway. She tried to be non-threatening and polite on the phone and asked some extra questions concerning the points offered by the Head of Human Resources.

In fact the call turned into quite a discussion of what comes over well at interview, particularly with regard to the presentation Sonia had carried out – which had not gone as well as she had hoped. Sonia found out that she came a close second in the interview, and the presentation was what had let her down. The organization was not sure if she had the capacity to improve on this area of her work, which would form a large part of the job.

She ended the call saying thank you: 'I really do appreciate the time you have spent on this feedback and I will certainly study what you have told me. I know it will help me make a better impression in the next job I go for.'

The Head of Human Resources rang her back shortly afterwards. Another similar vacancy had suddenly become available in the organization. They had been so impressed by Sonia's attitude in her phone call, and her determination to learn how to improve her presentations that Sonia was offered this new job on the spot. She had got herself the job she wanted as a direct result of the way that she handled that phone call to get feedback.

Of course, her great manner on the phone merely reflected her genuine desire to learn and improve – something that will always impress employers.

Learning and improving

If you regularly evaluate your presentations in this way it can become part of how you can build learning into experience.

Knockout Tip!

The way to improve any skill is to practise so it becomes second nature.

Practice makes perfect

Presentation skills are a highly useful skill to be able to offer in the employment market. It will benefit your future career if you can say that you are confident about speaking in public.

Many jobs involve speaking to clients, suppliers or customers; but even more, they involve speaking to colleagues, management or new members of staff. If you want to move on in your speaking career to enhance your employability there is one sure way of getting better: do more of it.

The more you expose yourself to the rigours of having to make presentations to groups of people, the better you will get. For a start, you will be more practised, which will mean unexpected events will throw you less. You will stand to gain more feedback on how you come across which will help you tailor your approach. You will pick up from the audience what works well and what could be improved. The only way to get better at a skill is to practise it.

Transferable skills

It is also worth saying that presentation skills are more than just skills for advancement at work – they are also vital skills for life. If you can create a message with flair, hold the floor and speak confidently, you will find you gain advantage in social and personal terms.

We are all attracted to confident, open, direct people who have things to say; these are the skills that you are developing, and being able to do a knockout presentation at interview can also make you a winner in many other areas of your life.

So resolve now to grab the chance to address groups when you can. See it as an opportunity to improve. Even better is to increase the size of the audience so that you get used to speaking to bigger crowds – say, at a work conference – as then, a small interview panel will seem easy-peasy in comparison. Even just participating more in meetings and seminars will give you more practice.

Giving and getting objective feedback

Once a presentation is done, it does not necessarily have to be over. If you have reliable friends or colleagues with more experience, you might consider talking through your evaluation sheets with them to see if they can give you any advice about what could have improved your contribution. After the interview and presentation are over, you will not mind talking about the experience with other people. Obviously you have to offer this kind of post-interview feedback to them in return.

Think widely and laterally about what can help you develop in this arena. If you get the chance to sum up at seminars or training sessions, do so. If a group needs someone to chair a meeting, offer your services. Have as your ultimate aim to become the kind of person who would be happy to speak to a group at very little notice.

Chairing skills

You may not think that chairing or leading a meeting is the same as giving a presentation but it involves you leading discussions, summing up key points, and directing the business of the meeting. All these skills are of direct relevance to making a presentation as they encourage you to be more assertive, speaking in front of a group. It also encourages other people to see you more as a confident leader – which can prove an asset if a job comes along which requires you to make a knockout presentation to the interview panel.

Career development

When you move on in your career you can help other people in turn. Ensure that you take the acquisition of presentation skills seriously if you ever become a manager or a supervisor. If you get the chance to put some skills training on the agenda, think of the ways that learning how to make a presentation in public can benefit your staff or workers.

Even if formal tuition is not an option, you can encourage healthy self- and peer-evaluation of how each member of the team is doing, and could set up events to provide people with practice delivering work presentations, and giving each other feedback.

In Chapter 6 we will look at the questions that people ask about presentations in interviews. They cover overcoming hurdles, handling nightmare situations and dealing with nerves. Even though those things do not happen often, they sometimes can, and to think them through in advance can help you cope, on the day when you face a difficulty.

Dos and don'ts

✔ Do challenge yourself to get better.

✔ Do think through every aspect of your presentation.

✔ Do be prepared to reinvent your approach if you were unsuccessful.

✘ Don't make snap judgements about how you have done.

✘ Don't get stuck in your ways – you need to keep innovating.

✘ Don't take criticism to heart – just treat it as professional advice.

Points to remember

1. It is very difficult to improve if you only give a presentation once in a while at a job interview, so try to build up your experience in-between times.

2. Think of your public-speaking career as a whole, and try to get experience of different types of presentation to a variety of audiences.

3. Feedback from the panel may give you a completely different perspective.

4. Feedback from trusted friends can help you to see the whole picture.

5. Never rest on your laurels, even if you do well at interview; you need to keep working on your presentation skills for the next time.

Facing tricky situations

Even the most thorough preparation can't predict every difficult situation that can arise. From technical failures to nervous dilemmas, disasters do happen and a selection of tricky issues is covered in this chapter. Finding yourself in front of the panel from hell and handling a variety of nightmare situations are considered.

Some common myths

People have funny ideas about doing presentations. Here are some of the most common – and untrue – myths.

○ Being nervous on the day will lose you the job:
  All candidates show signs of nerves. It is completely natural. On its own it will not lose you the job unless your nerves stop you talking entirely. Getting started often feels like the hardest, most nerve-racking part. Once you get going your nerves will get under control and all the wonderful planning and preparation you have done on your presentation will enable you to concentrate on the message and achieve your task.
  Many people who get jobs felt quite nervy throughout their presentations beforehand. Just do the best you can.

Nerves don't show nearly as much as you think they do. The sweating palms, churning stomach and knocking knees probably are never detected by the panel. They will expect a certain level of nerves as normal and will want to concentrate on what you have got to say.

○ You can be too smartly dressed for an interview:
Not unless you turn up in a ball gown or dinner jacket you can't. Being dressed at least slightly smarter than you would have to look in the job is expected. It shows that you have taken time and trouble over the way you look because you are keen to get the job. The best reason to dress up for an interview is because all the other candidates will and you will look a bit scruffy in comparison if you don't.

Panels think the job they have to offer is important. Even the most lowly job will pay thousands of pounds every year in wages. They want to know that you would value this opportunity highly, and making an effort with your appearance helps to demonstrate that. Think of it as just like going on a first date.

○ It looks odd if you don't use PowerPoint:
Not at all. The most important aspect of visual aids to consider is whether it adds to your presentation. Boring slides repeating every word you are saying will add nothing.

Often you can hear the panel sigh with relief after several identical PowerPoint presentations, when at last a candidate comes in and says, 'I don't have any slides. I am just going to talk about my ideas in this presentation. I have made a summary on this handout which I will give you at the end.'

○ You can't be expected to plan for a presentation when they are only going to give you the subject on the day:

Yes you can. You can set your mind to every possible question that might come up by combing through all the job material that you have been sent, looking at the organization's website and using all your critical faculties to second guess what might come up.

Don't leave yourself exposed by doing nothing, when you should be perfectly able to plan a skeleton response to a question which will be likely to give you a head start.

○ Structure isn't that important:
Yes it is! It's vital that you have an Introduction, a Conclusion, and three key points. Not seven key points or 25 key points, but three. It enables your audience to follow what you are saying – which gives you extra impact. It will stop you waffling and wandering around your material and ensures that you are clear, focused and pithy.

Questions and answers

However comprehensive a book on this topic may be, there will still be some questions left at the end. Here is a selection of the most often asked ones. The questions and answers section in this chapter responds to common problems and provides suggestions. Here you can find the answers to overcoming hurdles and coping with difficulties.

After you have read each question, pause before reading on, to see what answer *you* would recommend. Then read what I have answered, to see if you agree with what I have said.

1. Feelings of fear
   Q: 'Although I always prepare well, I have such a fear of drying up in the middle of my presentation, which makes me so nervous. Is there anything I can do to stop this happening?'

A: Yes, there is. You need to deal with this worry which is the hurdle most likely to trip you up. You need to stop predicting failure for yourself. A large part of success under pressure is down to a positive mental attitude. Any sports star will tell you that they feel that all their training can go down the drain unless they feel like a winner on the day.

Athletes call this technique 'envisaging' and it is thought to be very powerful. Many world class football teams and other sports people employ sports psychologists to help them stay buoyant and strong mentally when the pressure builds up. You can make this technique work for you too.

Spend some time the night before the interview just imagining yourself doing well. Have a waking dream where you imagine how you will feel walking in to do your presentation. Imagine how good you look and the great first impression you will make on the panel. See yourself smiling and shaking hands with them all. Think how you will act and behave when it is all going well. Think through the reaction of the audience on the panel, see them enjoying your presentation, paying you attention and congratulating you when you finish.

If you can create this positive scenario in your mind's eye, it can help see you through the real event which is to come, and indeed can also make a big difference to the outcome. You will literally be living your dream and living up to the high expectations you have set for yourself.

2. Answering questions

Q: 'I am quite confident doing my presentation as I know the material inside out. My problem is, I get really jittery at the questions because I can't predict what they are going to ask me. I fluff my answers even though when I recall them afterwards I can think of perfectly good responses then.'

A: Actually you can predict what they are going to ask you with a fair amount of accuracy. I think you need to put a bit less work into making your presentation totally perfect and spend more time estimating in advance what the questions could be.

For a start, revisit each of your previous interviews and see how many of the questions you have ever been asked, you can recall. Write them down, together with what you can remember of the answers you gave and what you would have liked to have said on reflection.

Evaluate the questions you have been asked compared to the presentations you have already given, and think through next time you have to give a presentation in your interview, what the likely areas of questioning might be.

By comparing the presentations and questions from the past, you may well be able to predict the kind of questions that often come up. Do the panel always ask for more information; for more detail; for you to explain how something works, or for you to take their understanding of your topic further? Do they ask for your opinion, or for you to summarize some point of your presentation?

See if there is any kind of pattern to the things you have been questioned on in the past. Perhaps your presentations have been so perfect that you are always asked about your feelings on the topic, in an effort by the panel to elicit some emotion or passion on the topic from you. Once you have found the pattern, you can either alter your style of presentation to include more of what they are looking for, or you can prepare in advance your answers to the questions you now know should come.

3. Blushing

Q: 'I blush when I get nervous. I know most people say it doesn't matter but mine is a really bad case. My face and neck go bright red straight away and I get so self-conscious that I feel I can't carry on. I look awful when it happens and I am sure that the panel can't believe how bad it gets.'

A: A job interview is not a beauty contest. Most people exhibit some kind of nervous symptom. You need to get yours into perspective. It is another symptom of the fight or flight mechanism which is causing this flushing, so is a purely rational response to the 'threat' of having to speak in public. It could be far worse. Imagine if your nerves stopped you talking at all or made you muddle up your words completely or prompted you to start crying. Your red rash is very minor in the general scheme of things.

Yes, the panel probably do notice that you go red in the neck and face but lots of people share this specific show of nervousness, possibly even including panel members themselves! It should not be dwelt on and what you are saying soon takes over their interest rather than looking at you changing colour. Get over it, ignore it and you will soon find the effects start to lessen.

4. Enemy on the panel

Q: 'For the last four years I have had a difficult relationship with someone at work. To my horror I have just found out that she is on my promotion interview panel. I am dreading it as I know she will mark me down and I am wondering whether to bother at all.'

A: Well, there are only a limited amount of choices open to you here. You could withdraw from the interview and then there certainly will be no promotion for you in that case. Or you could brave it out. Just consider for a second that you might be wrong and she might not have feelings either way about your ability. You could have misconstrued her opinion in the past or her views may have changed.

Even if she does not rate you very highly, if you do well, she may find a new respect for you and find that your presentation of your material is very impressive. So put the past behind you, enter the interview room with a neutral view of her, and show the panel how well you can perform and how much you have to offer.

5. Accent

Q: 'I am from Nigeria and am often told that my accent is difficult to understand. I can't change it and I sometimes wonder if it is just the fact that I am from a different racial group that they object to.'

A: You can't change the way you speak and you can't change your racial origins. It is illegal for anyone to discriminate against you on grounds of race. If you are worried that you may not be understood, you can try to speak slightly more slowly and clearly to give the panel more chance to 'tune in' to your accent.

You must not assume that they are going to be against you as this will show in your manner. Maintain an upbeat outlook and keep on trying to succeed. Make sure that you are not confusing not being understood with the panel not liking your presentation. Have you had feedback on how you came across? You may find that you can improve what you are saying rather than the way you present it.

6. Clothes

   Q: 'I don't know what to wear for an interview with a presentation. It is for a job where the tone is fairly casual but I feel I need to look a bit smarter than normal.'

   A: I think your instincts are right. If it is for a job where most people don't wear suits to work then just go to the interview in a plain dark jacket. Even if you look slightly smarter than you would in the job, it shows the panel (who will all be looking quite smart) that you have made an effort, that you are keen to make a good impression and that you understand the importance of having an impact on them.

7. Hair

   Q: 'I am female with long hair which looks nice (I have been told) but there is quite a lot of it as it is thick, long and curly. Should I tie it back?'

   A: Yes, as long as you can wear it comfortably and smartly that way. You need to feel at ease, but generally you will look more businesslike if you can tame your hair for the interview, and particularly when you are doing the presentation.

   I gave this advice a while back to a woman who was trying to get her first management job. She wore her hair like yours with great pride. She was outraged at my advice as she felt her hairstyle was a very important part of who she was. However, she was trying to advance her career so gave it a go and duly tied her hair back. She got the job and the panel told her afterwards that she just seemed much more purposeful and showed her leadership qualities that day.

   I still maintain they saw those aspects of her because her appearance was not distracting them.

8. Shoes

Q: 'Does the condition of your shoes really make such a difference? I resent having to buy new ones just for an interview.'

A: Yes it does, but that doesn't mean you should go out and buy a new pair of shoes tomorrow. A lot of people don't notice footwear, but every so often you will find someone who does. I know a very senior person in Government who says people's shoes are always the first thing he notices. 'I think it says a lot about a person, what shoes they wear', he says. 'They don't need to be new, but they do need to look good and be really, really clean.'

So there is the answer: clean the smartest pair of shoes you have – and I mean really clean them, with proper polish and a brush, until they shine – for each and every interview.

If you are buying a new pair, don't go for trendy, stylish shoes necessarily – comfort is important but so is looking businesslike and smart. Think, 'work shoes that I could carry on using if I get the job'.

9. Drinks

Q: 'I always refuse a drink of tea or coffee. Is this correct? I don't want the panel to think I am rude.'

A: You will often find a bottle or glass of water provided for you and it is fine to say no to a tea or coffee. It only gives you more to worry about and more to fumble with when you are already under stress. So skip the drink and concentrate on the message of your presentation. The panel will not even notice whether you partake or not but they will if you accept and then slop the coffee all down your interview suit.

10. Jewellery

Q: 'I have unusual piercings in my ears but I always wear earrings in them. Surely this isn't something a panel would notice?'

A: Yes they would. Take them out for the interview at least. This applies to anything else that you habitually wear, such as a hat, or your iPod or any particular accessory that you feel sums up your essential personality. It may be that you can wear them to work once you get the job but take it carefully to start with. The client group the company deals with may be a particularly conservative or traditional type, so you may need to rein in your individuality. You certainly don't need them on show in the interview.

When you are doing your presentation, the panel will be looking at you to see if they can imagine you holding the floor at gatherings of clients and customers. In the interview you need to look as though you would fit in and not scare the horses.

11. Humour

Q: 'I want to be funny in my presentations – at least occasionally – but I find it very awkward to try. I heard that women find it harder to be funny than men. Is this true?'

A: There are fewer female comics than male and there is less of a jokey group tradition between women, but that doesn't mean you can't learn how to lighten your presentations with humour. Make a big effort to bring in humorous comments or points in your work generally, to learn more about how to manage this. Read more books on this topic to inform you about tips and techniques.

12. Drugs

Q: 'In the past I have resorted to drugs to help me calm down. Not illegal ones, just holistic inhalers and calming remedies. I am not sure if they worked though. Is there anything you can recommend?'

A: I certainly don't suggest illegal drugs or drink before an interview. They may relax you but they will also slow you down and dull your responses. As for holistic or any other over-the-counter remedies, well, be sure of what you are taking, in case it makes you worse or has some side-effects. I have heard that eating a banana can help calm nerves but make sure you have finished it before being called in to do your presentation!

13. PowerPoint

Q: 'I have been asked to prepare a PowerPoint presentation for my interview. I have never used this program before and am getting nervous just thinking about it. Have you any tips?'

A: Yes, get practising. Find some time on a computer when you can range through the PowerPoint program and find your way around it. If you have a colleague or friend who can advise you, book some time with them. Once you have looked through how the program works you can start to plan what you want to do with it. It is a very user-friendly package so don't be scared.

Then you need to think what your vision is for your presentation. You presumably know what your topic is and what you are planning to include. You need a view of what your slides will say and what each will contain. For a short presentation of only a few minutes, I don't recommend much. Less is definitely more with PowerPoint and it is best used as a device to summarize what you are saying overall.

You can choose from the pre-prepared slides on PowerPoint or you can design your own. I would recommend the latter, keeping it simple and clear: just key points, dark lettering on a light background for visibility, and perhaps highlighting your bullet points in a light bright colour. However, technology can fail on the day, so even though you will have prepared your visual aids, take a spare copy with you and always be ready to perform without them if the computer lets you down.

14. Nerves

Q: 'My nerves are not like other people's. I don't just get flustered, I get completely lost, start sweating and stumble over my words, and at my last interview I was unable to carry on with my presentation. I just stopped about halfway through. I know this is restricting me being in the running for jobs, which is so annoying as I can do the job OK, but just can't keep my nerve during the interview.'

Knockout Tip!

Concentrating on the message you are giving will help you get over feeling self-conscious.

A: First, take a step back from this being the gateway to a new job, and re-define it as a chance to talk to people about your views on an aspect of the job. If you think of the presentation in the light of 'an opportunity' rather than as 'a threat', you can start to turn around your experience of it.

You need to get much more involved with your material. Really soak yourself in what you are going to say so that you can almost recite it without notes. You will be able to overcome a lot of your self-consciousness if you bother more with what you are saying than on the fact that people are looking at you.

You also need to switch on the knob in your head that says 'Override', so that you shrug off being the centre of attention and get on with the job you have to do on the day. You say that you can do the job fine if only they would offer it to you, but how are the members of the panel to know this if you can't get through one 15-minute presentation to them? I'm not unsympathetic to what you are saying but ultimately you are in control of how well you do. Even if you get tied up in knots, do not give up. You have to pick up the reins and carry on. Every single candidate in front of that panel will suffer from an attack of nerves as well, I can guarantee it.

Think to yourself: 'The panel need me to carry on, otherwise they will get anxious and be let down.' You need to externalize the need to finish, in order to create a positive gesture to the panel – as opposed to your relief at finishing early. All that is happening to you is that you are succumbing to the 'flight' part of the 'fight or flight mechanism'. I don't want you to start fighting with the panel either, but you do need to have a bit more determination to stand your ground and complete the task you have been given.

There are a couple of things you can do that will help you survive:
–   Before you start your presentation, make sure you have a glass of water near you. If you do temporarily dry up, a drink will help you and it gives you reason to have a short pause which is always perfectly acceptable.

– Again, before you start, take some deep breaths. Two or three extra intakes of breath can help to fuel your brain to override that blank feeling when every logical thought escapes you. I know this is the difficult bit but if you can just BREATHE deeply every time the fog descends, you will find the fog clears again after a couple of seconds.

Trust me. You can do this; just concentrate on the task you are going to complete, smile and get going.

15. Sit or stand?

Q: 'I have a repeat interview for a job (they didn't appoint anyone the first time) and there is a presentation as part of it. The panel is only three people and I sat down last time for my presentation. Are you really saying it would be better to stand up for it? I would be towering over the three of them.'

A: Yes. Stand up. Unless the room is tiny with just room for you, the table and them, it would look more authoritative if you stood. Did you get any feedback last time about why you were not picked for the job? Was any part of it that they were not sure if you were up to the demands of the job? Ensure that you maximize your authority this time.

16. Stammering

Q: 'Is there any help for someone with a stammer? I feel this is stopping me doing well at interviews as, obviously, doing a presentation affects me far more than doing a normal interview because I am in the spotlight.'

A: Try getting in touch with the British Stammering Association if you haven't already. They have a helpful website at www.stammering.org, with hints and tips from people who know.

One of the good elements of a presentation rather than the interview itself is that at least you are in charge of what you say in the presentation. You can choose which words to use and you can limit your likelihood of stammering that way. You can also rehearse before the event, which should enable you to devise strategies to help control your speech.

Always tell the panel before you start that you are sometimes affected by stammering, rather than letting them find out and feel anxious about it.

17. Over-preparation

Q: 'Is it possible to be over-prepared for an interview? I have done so much work on my presentation that I feel I am dreaming about it every night.'

A: It could be possible, but it is very unlikely. Normally, getting soaked in your subject is helpful as you will know your material inside out by the time of the interview. Any presentation should be focusing on information that is quite familiar to you anyway, as it is about the job that you are potentially going to do.

What you need to do is retain your enthusiasm and interest in the topic so that you can come across as keen and gripped by the subject. You can always introduce some fresh activity or element to your presentation near to the actual day if you are worried about it feeling stale.

18. Technology

Q: 'I am very nervous about using computers during my presentation. I have been told I can show visuals that way if I want to. Will it look bad if I don't?'

A: No. Just ensure that your material is easy to understand, your approach is fresh and lively, and your message clear. Only use a visual aid if there is some point to it, for example, adding weight to something you've already mentioned.

19. Concentration

Q: 'I write my structure out the way you told me to but when I deliver the presentation, I go off the point entirely. I end up waffling – on up to about nine different key points – and then run out of time. My prompt cards are neatly prepared but I don't seem able to keep to them.'

A: You have done well to put your presentation together in a structured way with three key points but you must have more discipline when you present them to the panel. When you introduce what you are going to do, I presume you tell your audience that you are going to tell them three key points. They must get totally confused when you proceed to tell them lots more than that.

The first thing to do is to actually read your cards, rather than just hold them in your hands. You need to find a way to keep yourself on track. One way is to make more use of signposting about exactly what you are doing.

When you have introduced what you are going to say, tell them that you are now going to start on your first key point. Then once that one has been said, say, 'That was the first of my three points. Now I am going to move on to the second.' Do the same thing as you move from the second to the third. In this way you will not be able to deviate much, as you are constantly telling the panel exactly where you are in your presentation.

At the end you can say something like, 'That was the last of my three key points. Let me conclude this presentation by saying...'. You will be disciplining yourself to stick to the plan that you have made, the audience will feel reassured that you are talking to them about what you said you were going to cover, and your presentation will be all the better for it.

You really do not want to wander all over the place with your material. For a start you will go way over your time, and secondly, it won't make so much sense. So think of your audience and how best you can help them by restraining yourself from nervously adding more and more points to your speech which really won't improve anything in the long run.

20. Voice

Q: 'My voice gets high and squeaky when I am nervous and I start gabbling ridiculously fast. I don't sound as though I am in control at all.'

A: That is because you aren't in control. The high squeaky voice is due to terror and the increasing speed is part of the flight response kicking in.

You are unconsciously hurrying to get it all over with as soon as possible. You can slow yourself down by calling on your conscious mind to help you. Write down on your prompt notes messages to yourself on this topic: 'Slow down here!' or 'Not so fast!' on each card. No one will see these secret instructions except you.

The pitch of your voice is more difficult to lower but you can try rehearsing with it a tone or two deeper. You need to open the back of your throat when you talk more. Practise and see. Slowing down and breathing deeply are the two best tips for increasing the authority of your voice.

Your questions

Did you find a question that you wanted answered in the list above? Perhaps you have more questions to which you would like a response on the topic of presentations in the interview. If so, contact me via my website on www.rebeccatee.com, and you could see your query answered in the next edition of this book.

Dos and don'ts

✔ Do read this book through next time you have an interview coming up.

✔ Do push yourself to develop your style and be ambitious for what you can achieve.

✔ Do prepare thoroughly – it is the key to giving your knockout performance.

✗ Don't lose your nerve. Everyone feels scared – it is quite normal.

✗ Don't give up if getting a job seems impossible. It will happen if you keep trying.

✗ Don't forget to take every chance you can to speak in public.

Points to remember

1. You will improve at presentations the more of them you do.

2. Every single candidate will be as nervous as you are.

3. When you know someone who has done an interview presentation, find out what they did and how it went.

4. There are always things you can improve, however well you do.

5. Someone has to get the job; next time it could be you.

Conclusion

The Conclusion sums up the contents of the book and provides you with a step-by-step guide to giving a knockout presentation in your interview. Further sources of help from Kogan Page are provided at the end of the book.

Checklist

Step 1: Get your head sorted

Your job may have been made redundant or you are trying for a new position whilst not feeling at your best, but you have to transform your attitude. Of all the parts of the selection process, delivering a presentation requires a confident approach. Even if you are feeling insecure and inadequate, you need to push these thoughts into the background so that only good emotions are present as you focus on making the best impression you can. *You* are in charge of how you feel so take the decision to banish all negative thoughts.

Step 2: Plan

Plan your presentation thoroughly. Whether you have been given your topic or have some possible ideas for an unseen subject, start with planning your answers. Research the job you are going for and the employing company; check out the audience for the presentation as far as you can, and get imaginative with your ideas for what you could include. Think about the venue and what kind of interview it is likely to be.

Use notes – in a spider diagram if possible – and plot your three main thoughts. Now let yourself focus on the whole picture to help you get creative, make associations, generate ideas, and to connect your thoughts into an overall shape. Keep coming back to this diagram as new ideas occur to you. At this stage don't restrict yourself and don't cut anything out. Use coloured pens to help you see your different ideas more clearly.

Now start to get selective about what three points you will have as the basis for your presentation and what information you might include about each of them. Get feedback on these early thoughts from trusted colleagues, friends or family.

Step 3: Prepare

Prepare all aspects carefully. Assume nothing until you have checked it all out. Structure what you want to say. This means disciplining yourself to three key points in the body of your presentation. Each of these could have its own three key points too. You need to shape an Introduction and a Conclusion to top and tail your work. Use the 'ham sandwich' boxes to lay out your structured presentation. This will make it much clearer to your audience. Do not be over-ambitious in what you include.

Avoid jargon and use appropriate language. That way you can be sure that everyone will understand what you are talking about. If you need to include technical terms, think how you can add explanations to make them understandable to lay people. Plan for misjudging the time and build in a couple of extra points that you can use if the time is available. Talking into a tape recorder is a good way of timing what you will say.

Spend adequate time rehearsing the material to generate your enthusiasm and confidence about what you are going to say. Have a dummy run through if you can find a quiet time at the venue. If that is not possible, practise making the presentation to friends, or at least in front of the mirror.

Summarize your whole presentation on cards, to use as your prompts. Establish what you are going to wear and get your outfit ready for the big day. For instant impact, dress one level more smartly than usual. Never wear anything distracting. You want the audience to focus on the message not the messenger.

Step 4: Present it

Vary the speed, tone and volume of your voice. Speak more slowly and clearly than in normal conversation. Express any concerns. The audience only knows what you tell them – they can't see your prompt notes so don't worry about sticking to every word. Show passion if it is appropriate, and enthusiasm when you can.

Do not let nerves hold you back. Before you go on stage, find a place to be alone and slowly say the vowel sounds 'A – E – I – O – U', making your mouth stretch as much as possible whilst doing so. This limbers up the face muscles to enable you to speak as you have planned, and to enunciate clearly. Take a few deep breaths before speaking and stand straight with your shoulders back. Have a glass of water beside you in case your mouth becomes dry.

Always smile when you greet and leave your audience – you want to be noticed and to hold the audience's attention. Stand tall, take up a lot of space and remember, you are *performing*. Make sure you introduce yourself and your subject in every presentation – even when you think that people know you and why you are there.

Add variety to your tone to keep the audience alert. Do not rush your words – most people speak too fast under pressure. Pauses can be very powerful as they add emphasis to your speech and allow you time to collect your thoughts while the audience is catching up with what has just been said. Do not try to put on a fancy voice or a different way of speaking, but do speak more slowly and clearly than in normal conversation.

You will not be able to look at everyone, but remember to glance around the audience (use the 'M' or 'W' shape) when you can. You want to give the impression that you are relating to every member of the panel. Try to end on an upbeat note, and include personal examples where possible.

Concentrate on the importance of your message; authority comes from confidence. Giving a presentation is a privilege, and enthusiasm or passion often carry the day.

Step 5: Get feedback

Get feedback to see how you did and to give you points to work on. Reflect on the way you do your presentations, learn from watching other people and stay determined to develop further. You have all the tools and advice for a great interview presentation at your fingertips. Now go and be a knockout.

Golden rules

- Make it happen – be positive.
- Plan thoroughly.
- Keep it simple.
- Structure your presentation.
- Use friends and family for rehearsals.
- Breathe, and slow down.

○ Just do it (practice makes perfect).

○ Get feedback.

For more advice on interviews generally, see my companion book, *Successful Interview Skills*, 5th edition, by Rebecca Corfield, published by Kogan Page, 2009.

Further reading from Kogan Page

Advanced IQ Tests
ISBN 978 0 7494 5232 2
The Advanced Numeracy Test Workbook
ISBN 978 0 7494 5406 7
Aptitude, Personality & Motivation Tests
ISBN 978 0 7494 5651 1
The Aptitude Test Workbook
ISBN 978 0 7494 5237 7
A-Z of Careers & Jobs
ISBN 978 0 7494 5510 1
Careers After the Armed Forces
ISBN 978 0 7494 5530 9
Career, Aptitude & Selection Tests
ISBN 978 0 7494 5695 5
Graduate Psychometric Test Workbook
ISBN 978 0 7494 5405 0
Great Answers to Tough Interview Questions
ISBN 978 0 7494 5196 7
How to Master Nursing Calculations
ISBN 978 0 7494 5162 2
How to Master Psychometric Tests
ISBN 978 0 7494 5165 3

How to Pass Advanced Aptitude Tests
ISBN 978 0 7494 5236 0
How to Pass Advanced Numeracy Tests
ISBN 978 0 7494 5229 2
How to Pass Advanced Verbal Reasoning Tests
ISBN 978 0 7494 4969 8
How to Pass the Civil Service Qualifying Tests
ISBN 978 0 7494 4853 0
How to Pass Data Interpretation Tests
ISBN 978 0 7494 4970 4
How to Pass Diagrammatic Reasoning Tests
ISBN 978 0 7494 4971 1
How to Pass the BMAT
ISBN 978 0 7494 5461 6
How to Pass the GMAT
ISBN 978 0 7494 4459 4
How to Pass Graduate Psychometric Tests
ISBN 978 0 7494 4852 3
How to Pass Numeracy Tests
ISBN 978 0 7494 5706 8
How to Pass Numerical Reasoning Tests
ISBN 978 0 7494 4796 0
How to Pass the Police Selection System
ISBN 978 0 7494 5712 9
How to Pass Professional Level Psychometric Tests
ISBN 978 0 7494 4207 1
How to Pass the QTS Numeracy Skills Test
ISBN 978 0 7494 5460 9
How to Pass Selection Tests
ISBN 978 0 7494 5693 1
How to Pass Technical Selection Tests
ISBN 978 0 7494 4375 7
How to Pass the UKCAT
ISBN 978 0 7494 5333 6
How to Pass the UK's National Firefighter Selection Process
ISBN 978 0 7494 5161 5

How to Pass Verbal Reasoning Tests
ISBN 978 0 7494 5696 2
How to Succeed at an Assessment Centre
ISBN 978 0 7494 5688 7
IQ and Aptitude Tests
ISBN 978 0 7494 4931 5
IQ and Personality Tests
ISBN 978 0 7494 4954 4
IQ and Psychometric Tests
ISBN 978 0 7494 5106 6
IQ and Psychometric Test Workbook
ISBN 978 0 7494 4378 8
IQ Testing
ISBN 978 0 7494 5642 9
The Numeracy Test Workbook
ISBN 978 0 7494 4045 9
Preparing the Perfect Job Application
ISBN 978 0 7494 5653 5
Preparing the Perfect CV
ISBN 978 0 7494 5654 2
Readymade CVs
ISBN 978 0 7494 5323 7
Readymade Job Search Letters
ISBN 978 0 7494 5322 0
Succeed at IQ Tests
ISBN 978 0 7494 5228 5
Successful Interview Skills
ISBN 978 0 7494 5652 8
Test and Assess Your Brain Quotient
ISBN 978 0 7494 5416 6
Test and Assess Your IQ
ISBN 978 0 7494 5234 6
Test Your EQ
ISBN 978 0 7494 5535 4
Test Your IQ
ISBN 978 0 7494 5677 1

Test Your Numerical Aptitude
ISBN 978 0 7494 5064 9
Test Your Own Aptitude
ISBN 978 0 7494 3887 6
Ultimate Aptitude Tests
ISBN 978 0 7494 5267 4
Ultimate Cover Letters
ISBN 978 0 7494 5328 2
Ultimate CV
ISBN 978 0 7494 5327 5
Ultimate Interview
ISBN 978 0 7494 5387 9
Ultimate IQ Tests
ISBN 978 0 7494 5309 1
Ultimate Job Search
ISBN 978 0 7494 5388 6
Ultimate Psychometric Tests
ISBN 978 0 7494 5308 4
Verbal Reasoning Test Workbook
ISBN 978 0 7494 5150 9

Sign up to receive regular e-mail updates on Kogan Page books at **www.koganpage.com/signup.aspx** and visit our website: www.koganpage.com